Fodor's POCKET 2001

sydney

Excerpted from *Fodor's Australia 2001*

fodor's travel publications
new york • toronto • london • sydney • auckland
www.fodors.com

contents

On the Road with Fodor's *iv*

Don't Forget to Write *v*

introducing sydney 2

here and there 10

eating out 86

shopping 108

outdoor activities and sports 116

nightlife and the arts 122

where to stay 130

practical information 142

index 171

maps

australia *vi–vii*

central sydney *viii–ix*

sydney harbour 14

the rocks and harbour bridge 22

macquarie street and the domain 36

sydney suburbs 52–53

greater sydney 71

sydney beaches 78–79

central sydney dining 91

sydney area dining 105

central sydney lodging 134–135

ON THE ROAD WITH FODOR'S

EVERY TRIP IS A SIGNIFICANT TRIP. Acutely aware of that fact, we've pulled out all stops in preparing *Fodor's Pocket Sydney*. To guide you in putting together your Sydney experience, we've created multiday itineraries and regional tours. And to direct you to the places that are truly worth your time and money, we've rallied the team of endearingly picky know-it-alls we're pleased to call our writers. Having seen all corners of Sydney, they're real experts. If you knew them, you'd poll them for tips yourself.

As the restaurant reviewer for the *Sydney Morning Herald*, food columnist for *Vogue Entertaining and Travel*, and co-editor of the *Sydney Morning Herald Good Food Guide*, **Terry Durack** is Australia's most influential food critic. He has written five cookbooks, including the widely acclaimed *Yum: A Voyage Around My Stomach*, and the just-released *Noodle*. He also writes a Sunday column for the *London Independent*.

British by birth, American by education, and Australian since 1979—after a stint as a Kiwi, as well—**Michael Gebicki** is a freelance travel writer and photographer now based in Sydney. Dashing articles about his global wanderings appear regularly in travel publications in North America, Europe, and Asia.

Don't Forget to Write

Keeping a travel guide fresh and up-to-date is a big job. So we love your feedback—positive and negative—and follow up on all suggestions. Contact the *Pocket Sydney* editor at editorsfodors.com or c/o Fodor's, 280 Park Avenue, New York, New York 10017. And have a wonderful trip!

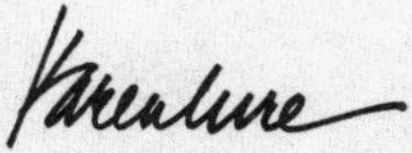

Karen Cure
Editorial Director

australia

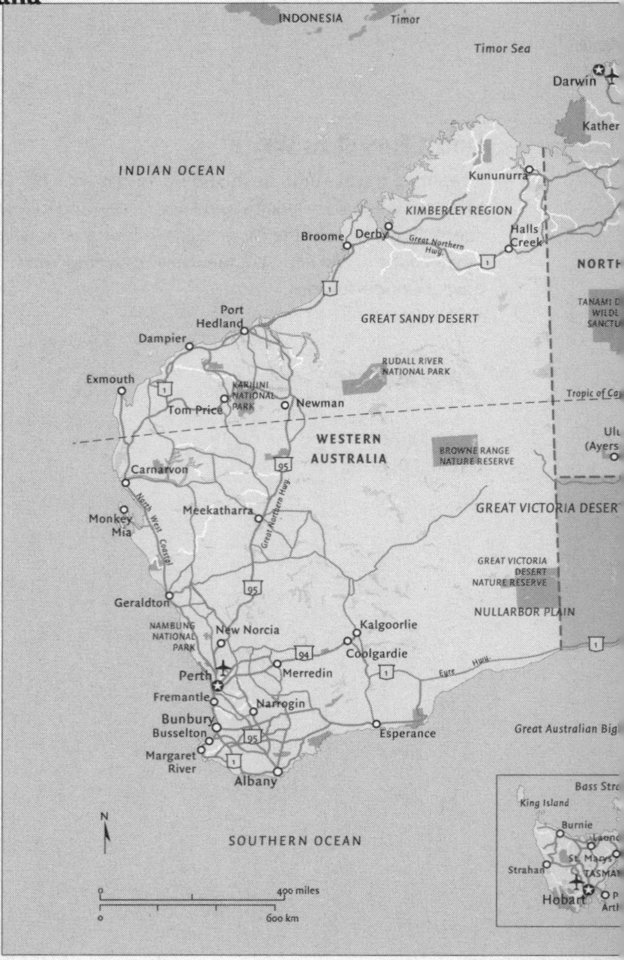
INDONESIA
Timor
Timor Sea
Darwin
Kather
INDIAN OCEAN
Kununurra
KIMBERLEY REGION
Halls Creek
Broome
Derby
Great Northern Hwy.
NORTH
TANAMI D
WILDE
SANCTU
Port Hedland
GREAT SANDY DESERT
Dampier
RUDALL RIVER NATIONAL PARK
Exmouth
KARIJINI NATIONAL PARK
Tom Price
Newman
Tropic of Ca
WESTERN AUSTRALIA
BROWNE RANGE NATURE RESERVE
Ulu
(Ayers
Carnarvon
North West Coastal
Monkey Mia
Meekatharra
Great Northern Hwy.
GREAT VICTORIA DESER
GREAT VICTORIA DESERT NATURE RESERVE
NULLARBOR PLAIN
Geraldton
NAMBUNG NATIONAL PARK
New Norcia
Kalgoorlie
Coolgardie
Perth
Merredin
Eyre Hwy.
Fremantle
Narrogin
Bunbury
Busselton
Esperance
Great Australian Big
Margaret River
Albany
Bass Stra
King Island
Burnie
Launc
St. Marys
Strahan
TASMA
Hobart
Arth
N
SOUTHERN OCEAN
0
400 miles
0
600 km

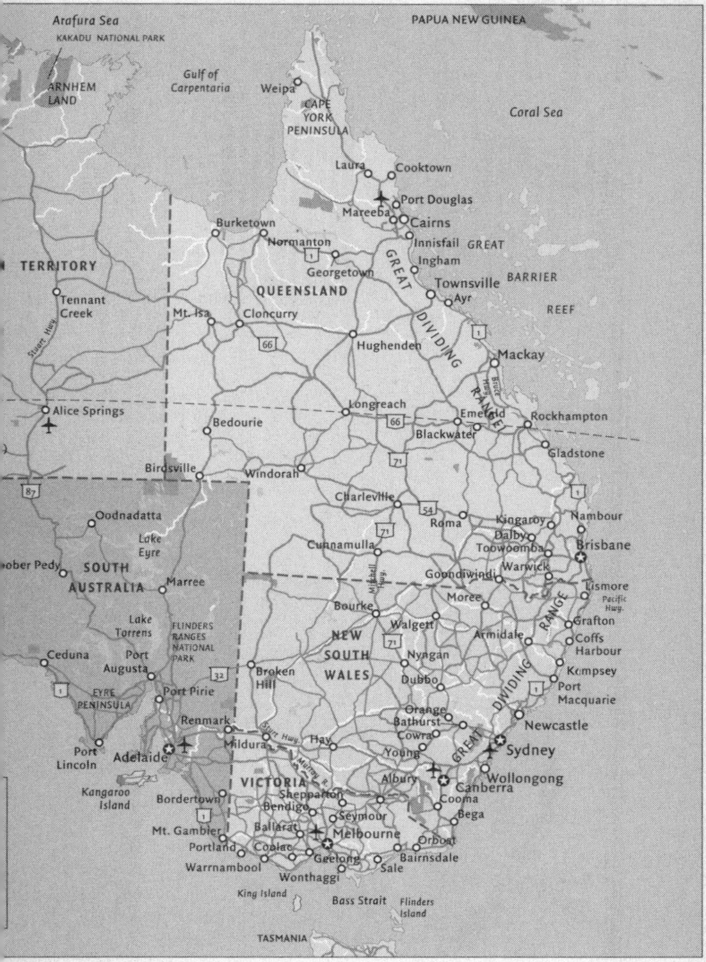
Arafura Sea
KAKADU NATIONAL PARK
ARNHEM LAND
Gulf of Carpentaria
Weipa
CAPE YORK PENINSULA
PAPUA NEW GUINEA
Coral Sea
Laura
Cooktown
Port Douglas
Mareeba
Cairns
Burketown
Normanton
Innisfail
GREAT BARRIER REEF
Ingham
Georgetown
TERRITORY
Townsville
Ayr
QUEENSLAND
Tennant Creek
Mt. Isa
Cloncurry
Stuart Hwy.
Hughenden
GREAT DIVIDING RANGE
Mackay
Bruce Hwy.
Longreach
Alice Springs
Emerald
Rockhampton
Bedourie
Blackwater
Gladstone
Birdsville
Windorah
Charleville
Roma
Kingaroy
Nambour
Oodnadatta
Dalby
Brisbane
Lake Eyre
Cunnamulla
Toowoomba
Warwick
Coober Pedy
SOUTH AUSTRALIA
Goondiwindi
Marree
Mitchell Hwy.
Lismore
Moree
Pacific Hwy.
Bourke
Walgett
Grafton
Lake Torrens
FLINDERS RANGES NATIONAL PARK
NEW SOUTH WALES
Armidale
Coffs Harbour
Ceduna
Port Augusta
Nyngan
Kempsey
Broken Hill
Dubbo
Port Macquarie
EYRE PENINSULA
Port Pirie
Orange
Bathurst
Newcastle
Renmark
Cowra
Sturt Hwy.
Hay
Sydney
Mildura
Young
Port Lincoln
Adelaide
Murray R.
Wollongong
VICTORIA
Albury
Canberra
Kangaroo Island
Shepparton
Cooma
Bordertown
Bendigo
Seymour
Bega
Mt. Gambier
Ballarat
Melbourne
Orbost
Portland
Colac
Geelong
Bairnsdale
Warrnambool
Sale
Wonthaggi
King Island
Bass Strait
Flinders Island
TASMANIA

central sydney

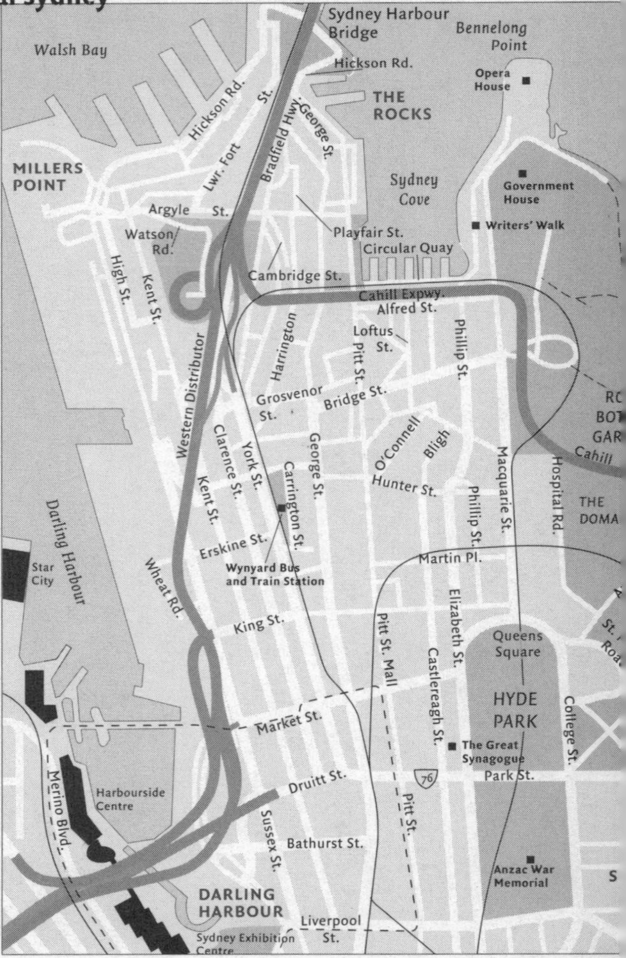
Sydney Harbour Bridge
Bennelong Point
Walsh Bay
Hickson Rd.
Opera House
THE ROCKS
Hickson Rd.
St.
Bradfield Hwy.
George St.
MILLERS POINT
Lwr. Fort
Sydney Cove
Government House
Argyle
St.
Watson Rd.
Playfair St.
Writers' Walk
Circular Quay
High St.
Kent St.
Cambridge St.
Cahill Expwy.
Alfred St.
Loftus St.
Harrington
Pitt St.
Phillip St.
Western Distributor
Grosvenor St.
Bridge St.
Clarence St.
York St.
George St.
O'Connell
Bligh
Macquarie St.
Hospital Rd.
Cahill
Kent St.
Carrington St.
Hunter St.
Phillip St.
THE DOMA
Darling Harbour
Star City
Erskine St.
Wynyard Bus and Train Station
Martin Pl.
Wheat Rd.
King St.
Pitt St. Mall
Elizabeth St.
Queens Square
Castlereagh St.
HYDE PARK
College St.
Market St.
The Great Synagogue
Park St.
Merino Blvd.
Harbourside Centre
Druitt St.
76
Pitt St.
Sussex St.
Bathurst St.
Anzac War Memorial
DARLING HARBOUR
Liverpool St.
Sydney Exhibition Centre

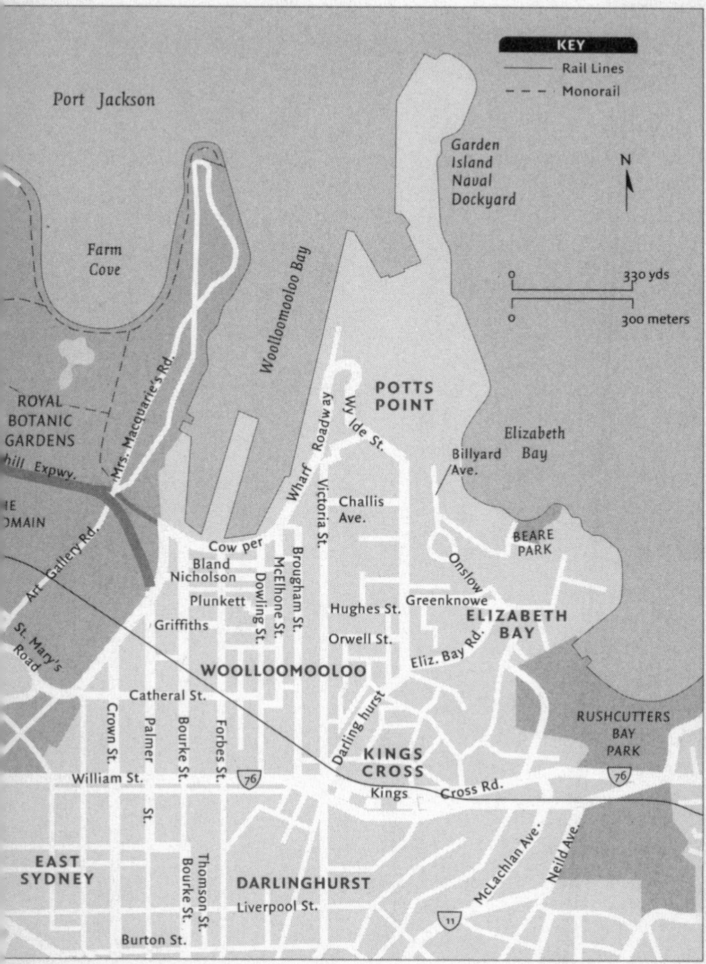

KEY
Rail Lines
Monorail
Port Jackson
Garden Island Naval Dockyard
N
0
330 yds
0
300 meters
Farm Cove
Woolloomooloo Bay
ROYAL BOTANIC GARDENS
Mrs. Macquarie's Rd.
POTTS POINT
Wylde St.
Wharf Roadway
Elizabeth Bay
Billyard Ave.
hill Expwy.
HE DOMAIN
Victoria St.
Challis Ave.
Art Gallery Rd.
Cowper
Bland
Nicholson
McElhone St.
Brougham St.
Dowling St.
BEARE PARK
Onslow
Plunkett
Greenknowe
Hughes St.
ELIZABETH BAY
Griffiths
Orwell St.
Eliz. Bay Rd.
St. Mary's Road
WOOLLOOMOOLOO
Catheral St.
Darling hurst
RUSHCUTTERS BAY PARK
Crown St.
Palmer St.
Bourke St.
Forbes St.
KINGS CROSS
76
William St.
Kings Cross Rd.
76
McLachlan Ave.
Neild Ave.
EAST SYDNEY
Thomson St.
Bourke St.
DARLINGHURST
Liverpool St.
11
Burton St.

sydney

In This Chapter

PLEASURES AND PASTIMES 5 • Beaches and Waterways 5 • Dining 5 • National Parks and Wildlife 6 • Sports 7 • Shopping 7 • QUICK TOURS 7 • Tour One 8 • Tour Two 8 • Tour Three 8 • Tour Four 9 • When to Tour Sydney 9

Updated by Michael Gebicki

introducing sydney

TAKE A TAXI FROM SYDNEY AIRPORT and chances are that the driver will not say "G'day" with the broad accent you might expect. Probe a little farther and you will probably discover that he was not born in Australia. Like the United States, Australia is a society of immigrants, and Sydney has been a preferred destination for many of these new arrivals. Over the past half century the Anglo-Irish immigrants who made up the city's original population base have been joined by successive waves of Italians, Greeks, Turks, Lebanese, and more recently, Asians. Today more than half of all Australians were either born overseas or have at least one parent who was. This intermingling has created a cultural vibrancy and energy that were missing only a generation ago.

Sydney is a city in a hurry. Compared with traffic in the rest of Australia, Sydney's is fast and impatient. The more than 4 million people in this city work hard and play harder. Moderation is something practiced by the citizens of Melbourne. Sydney has the tallest buildings, the most expensive real estate, the finest beaches, and the seediest nightlife of any Australian city. Most Australians regard its loud, brash ways with a mixture of fear and fascination, although Sydneysiders prefer to think of their city as virile rather than vulgar.

British writer Lawrence Durrell once lamented that Americans seem to live out of sync with their natural surroundings. The same could be said of Sydney's inhabitants. For the average Sydneysider, life unfolds in one of the red-roofed suburbs that surround the city. The outback is as foreign to most Sydneysiders as the Mojave Desert is to the inhabitants of Boston.

Sydney may have forsaken its hinterland, but it embraces its harbor with passion. The harbor is a shining gem, studded with small bays and inlets and crowned by the billowing sails of the Opera House. When he first set eyes on this harbor on 26 January 1788, Captain Arthur Phillip, the commander of the First Fleet, wrote in his diary: "We had the satisfaction of finding the finest harbor in the world, in which a thousand ships of the line may ride in the most perfect security." It was not an easy beginning, however. Passengers on board the 11 ships of the First Fleet were not the "huddled masses yearning to breathe free" who populated the United States, but wretched inmates flushed from overcrowded jails in England and sent halfway around the globe. It says much of those early days that when the women prisoners came ashore two weeks after the men, an orgy ensued.

Sydney has long since outgrown the stigma of its convict origins, but the passage of time has not tamed its spirit. Other Australian cities may lay claim to the title of the nation's cultural capital, but Sydney's panache and appetite for life are unchallenged. A walk among the scantily clad bathers at Bondi Beach or through the raucous nightlife district of Kings Cross provides evidence enough.

Visiting Sydney is an essential part of an Australian experience, but the city is no more representative of Australia than New York is of the United States. Sydney has joined the ranks of the great cosmopolitan cities whose characters are essentially international. What Sydney has to offer is style, sophistication, and great looks—an exhilarating prelude to the unique continent that lies at its back door.

PLEASURES AND PASTIMES

Although Sydney is well endowed with galleries, museums, and some splendid examples of Georgian and Victorian architecture, its warm climate, beaches, and outdoor activities are its prime attractions. Set against this sunny backdrop, Sydney offers an exciting choice of restaurants and cafés and a cosmopolitan array of shopping.

BEACHES AND WATERWAYS

The boom of the surf could well be Sydney's summer theme song: forty beaches, including world-famous Bondi, lie within the Sydney metropolitan area. Since Sidneysiders live with fine golden sand, an average water temperature of 68°F, and the choice of sheltered harbor waters or crashing breakers, it's little wonder they are addicted to the pleasures of sun, sea, and surfing.

The city is also a paradise for other water-based activities. A journey around Sydney Harbour reveals a natural wonderland of beaches, sheltered coves, high cliffs, and bays, which are ideal for boating, sailing, windsurfing, and diving. You can rent watercraft of all types or join a chartered sailing excursion to explore these delightful waters.

DINING

In the new world order, Sydney has suddenly become one of the glamorous global food centers, ranking up there with London and New York. Sydney-trained chefs are making their presence felt as far away as Great Britain, and Australian food magazines are giddy about what's going on at home.

So what's to eat in Sydney? There's tuna tartare with flying fish roe and wasabi; emu prosciutto; five-spice duck; shiitake-mushroom pie; and sweet turmeric barramundi curry. This is the stuff of mod-Oz (modern-Australian) cooking, and Sydney is where it flourishes, fueled by local produce and guided by

Mediterranean and Asian techniques. Sydney's dining scene is now as sunny and cosmopolitan as the city itself, and there are diverse and exotic culinary adventures to suit every appetite. A meal at Tetsuya's, Banc, or Rockpool constitutes a crash course in this dazzling culinary language.

Food lovers on holiday in Sydney are especially in luck, for many of Sydney's top sightseeing spots are of equal food interest. The Opera House has the Bennelong, and the Rocks has MCA Café. Then there are the food burbs of Bondi, Leichhardt, Surry Hills, and Darlinghurst, where the smells of good espresso, sizzling grills, or aromatic stir-fry hover in the air.

Seafood is a highlight. You'll find a variety of fish and shellfish that nearly boggles the mind: rudder fish, barramundi, blue-eye cod, kingfish, John Dory, ocean perch, and parrot fish; then Yamba prawns, Balmain bugs, sweet Sydney rock oysters, mud crab, spanner crab, yabbies (small lobsters), and marrons (freshwater lobsters). A visit to the city's fish markets at Pyrmont, just five minutes from the city center, will tell you much about Sydney's diet.

Of course, Sydney food tastes so much better when taken outdoors at a sidewalk table, in a sun-drenched courtyard, or best of all, in full view of that glorious harbor. Keep in mind the general rule: the better the view, the bigger the bill.

NATIONAL PARKS AND WILDLIFE

Anyone who wishes to sample the sights and sounds of wild Australia or experience the country's Aboriginal heritage can choose from several national parks (and numerous nature reserves) in the Greater Sydney region. Close to the heart of the city, Sydney Harbour National Park provides a habitat for many native species of plants and animals that are found nowhere else on earth. Ku-ring-gai Chase National Park to the north and Royal National Park to the south encompass large tracts of wild coastline and bushland.

SPORTS

Whether it's watching or playing, Sydneysiders are devoted to sports, and the city's benign climate makes outdoor sports a year-round possibility. There are some 80 golf courses within easy reach of the city. Many of these are open to the public, and greens fees are moderate. Tennis is also popular, and dozens of centers rent out courts for day and night use.

By far the most popular summer sport is cricket. Australia plays international test matches against England, the West Indies, Sri Lanka, Pakistan, South Africa, and India at the Sydney Cricket Ground. The biggest winter game is rugby league, but rugby union and Australian-rules football also attract passionate followings. Many of these winter matches take place at the Sydney Football Stadium.

SHOPPING

Sydney is a great place to shop for knitwear and woolen goods, sheepskin items, Aboriginal art and artifacts, opals, crafts, and innovative beach, leisure, and resort wear (raised to a virtual art form in this city of beaches). There are also plenty of outlets for local clothing designers, ranging from high fashion to bush- and country-wear manufacturers. Look for such names as Carla Zampatti, Hot Tuna, Collette Dinnigan, Country Road, Marcs, Lisa Ho, and Adele Weiss. Duty-free shops are plentiful, but the only real bargains apply to alcohol and tobacco products.

QUICK TOURS

If you're here for just a short period you need to plan carefully so you don't miss the must-see sights. The following itineraries will help you structure your visit efficiently. See Here and There for more information about individual sights.

TOUR ONE

For one of the best impressions of the city, head for Wharf 4 at Circular Quay and take either the Morning Harbour Cruise, which departs daily at 10 AM and 11:15 AM, or the Afternoon Harbour Cruise, which departs at 1 PM on weekdays and 1:30 PM on weekends. Follow the cruise with a walking tour of the historic Rocks, the nation's birthplace. If your trip falls on a weekend, visit The Rocks Market on Upper George Street for great souvenirs. End your tour at Campbell's Cove for a gorgeous view of the Sydney Opera House.

TOUR TWO

Walk past the Circular Quay ferry terminal to the Sydney Opera House. Take the stairs to the tour office on the lower forecourt level and join a guided one-hour tour. (Tours depart at frequent intervals from 9:15 to 4 on most days.) Afterwards, continue along the Farm Cove pathway, which skirts the edge of the Royal Botanic Gardens. Continue to Mrs. Macquarie's Point, which has exceptional views of the Opera House and Harbour Bridge. You can grab a bite at the Botanic Gardens Restaurant or at the café below. Walk back to the city through the gardens. Just before Macquarie Street, detour toward Government House and stroll through the gardens surrounding the house (open 10–4).

TOUR THREE

Take a taxi or catch Bus 311 from Alfred Street to Oxford Street in Paddington. Just past the long sandstone wall of Victoria Barracks on your right, hop off at Paddington Town Hall, the imposing Victorian building at the corner of Oatley Road. Continue along Oxford Street on foot, passing Juniper Hall. If you're there on a Saturday, walk to St. John's Church and browse through the stalls of Paddington Bazaar. Head down one of the side streets to view the pretty terrace houses of this suburb; notice their decorative balconies trimmed with Paddington lace. You can take a bus back to the city from the other side of

Oxford Street. If time remains, though, consider making the 20-minute trip on Bus 380 to Bondi Beach for a stroll along Australia's most famous strip of seashore.

TOUR FOUR

Take the monorail from the Market Street end of Pitt Street Mall to Darling Harbour (Darling Park stop) where you can explore the amusement parks, theaters, stores, and museums that line the waterfront. If time is restricted, the Sydney Aquarium offers the biggest thrills in the shortest time. Several of the sights here close at 5 PM, so plan accordingly. If you have another hour, take the Light Rail to Star City just west of Darling Harbour to view Sydney's Las Vegas–style casino. Return via Light Rail to Chinatown, south of the Chinese Garden. The area has a vast array of Oriental restaurants and food stalls, many at budget prices.

WHEN TO TOUR SYDNEY

The best times to visit Sydney are late spring and early fall. October and November are pleasantly warm, although the ocean is a bit too cold for swimming. December through February is hot and humid, with fierce tropical downpours in January and February. In March and April, weather is typically stable and comfortable, outdoor city life is still in full swing, and the ocean is at its warmest.

In This Chapter

SYDNEY HARBOUR 11 • A Good Cruise 12 • Sights to See 15 • THE ROCKS AND SYDNEY HARBOUR BRIDGE 20 • A Good Walk 21 • Sights to See 25 • MACQUARIE STREET AND THE DOMAIN SOUTH 32 • A Good Walk 33 • Sights to See 37 • THE OPERA HOUSE, THE RBG, AND THE DOMAIN NORTH 44 • A Good Walk 44 • Sights to See 46 • DARLING HARBOUR 50 • A Good Walk 50 • Sights to See 54 • SYDNEY CITY CENTER 56 • A Good Walk 56 • Sights to See 58 • ELIZABETH BAY AND KINGS CROSS, DARLINGHURST, AND PADDINGTON 61 • A Good Walk 61 • Sights to See 64 • AROUND SYDNEY 67 • Sights to See 68 • BEACHES 76 • Inside the Harbor 77 • South of the Harbor 80 • North of the Harbor 82

Updated by Michael Gebicki

here and there

SYDNEY IS A GIANT, stretching almost 97 km (60 mi) from top to bottom and about 55 km (34 mi) across. It is divided into north and south by the harbor, with most of the headline attractions located on the south shore. The area bounded by Chinatown in the south, the Harbour Bridge in the north, Darling Harbour to the west, and the beaches and coastline to the east has plenty to occupy any visitor for several days. North of the Harbour Bridge lie the important commercial center of North Sydney and the pleasant, leafy north-shore suburbs. Ocean beaches, Taronga Zoo, and Ku-ring-gai Chase National Park are the only reasons most visitors find to venture north of the harbor.

Numbers in the text correspond to numbers in the margin and on the Sydney Harbour, The Rocks and Harbour Bridge, Macquarie Street and the Domain, Sydney Suburbs, Greater Sydney, and Sydney Beaches maps.

SYDNEY HARBOUR

Captain Arthur Phillip, commander of the first European fleet to sail into these waters, called Sydney Harbour "in extent and security, very superior to any other that I have ever seen—containing a considerable number of coves, formed by narrow necks of land, mostly rocks, covered with timber." Two centuries later, few would dispute that the harbor is one of nature's extraordinary creations.

Officially titled Port Jackson, the harbor is in its depths a river valley carved by the Parramatta and Lane Cove rivers and the many creeks that flow in from the north. The rising sea level at the end of the last Ice Age submerged the floor of the valley, leaving only the walls. In the earliest days of the colony, the military laid claim to much of the harbor's 240 km (149 mi) of shoreline. Few of these military areas were ever fortified or cleared, and as a result, much of the foreshore has survived in its natural splendor. Several pockets of land are now protected within Sydney Harbour National Park. Such areas as North, South, and Middle Heads and the harbor islands that you'll pass on the harbor cruise are still much as they were in Governor Phillip's day.

This tour is based on the route followed by the State Transit Authority ferries on their daily Afternoon Harbour Cruise (☞ Practical Information). The Coffee Cruise run by Captain Cook Cruises follows a similar course. The tour takes in the eastern half of the harbor, from the city to the Heads and Middle Harbour. This is the glamorous side of the waterway, but the western shore has its own areas of historic and natural distinction, as well as Homebush Bay, which was the main site for the Olympic Summer Games in 2000 (☞ Sydney Olympic Park in Around Sydney, *below*).

A Good Cruise

As the vessel leaves the ferry wharves at Circular Quay, it crosses **Sydney Cove** ①, where the ships of the First Fleet dropped anchor in January 1788. After rounding Bennelong Point (named after an early Aboriginal inhabitant who was a favorite of Governor Phillip), site of the Sydney Opera House, the boat turns east and crosses **Farm Cove** ②, passing the Royal Botanic Gardens. The tall Gothic Revival chimneys just visible above the trees belong to Government House, the former official residence of the state governor.

GARDEN ISLAND ③, the country's largest naval dockyard, is easily identifiable across Woolloomooloo (say "*wool*-uh-muh-loo") Bay by its squadrons of sleek gray warships. Darling Point is the next headland, dominated by several tall apartment blocks and marking the beginning of Sydney's desirable eastern suburbs. Across Double Bay, **Point Piper** ④ is famous as the ritziest address in the country. The large expanse of water to the east of Point Piper is **Rose Bay** ⑤, bordered by another highly desirable, but somewhat more affordable, harborside suburb.

Beyond Rose Bay, **Vaucluse** ⑥ is yet another suburb that conveys social stature. The area is named after **Vaucluse House,** the sandstone mansion built by 19th-century explorer, publisher, and politician William Wentworth. The house is hidden from view, but you can see the Grecian columns of Strickland House, which was used as a convalescent home until a few years ago. To the east is Shark Bay, part of **Nielsen Park** and one of the most popular of the harbor bathing beaches (☞ Inside the Harbor *in* Beaches, *below*). **Watsons Bay** ⑦, a former fishing village, is the easternmost suburb on the harbor's south side. Beyond, the giant sandstone buttress of South Head rises high above the crashing Pacific breakers.

North Head is the boat's next landmark, followed by the beachside suburb of Manly (☞ Around Sydney, *below*), and the **Quarantine Station** ⑧. Once used to protect Sydney from disease, the station is a remnant from a fascinating chapter in the nation's history. The vessel then enters **Middle Harbour** ⑨—formed by creeks that spring from the forested peaks of Ku-ring-gai Chase National Park (☞ Around Sydney, *below*)—where you'll pass the beach at Clontarf on the right side of the vessel and sail through the Spit Bridge. After exploring Middle Harbour, you'll cruise by the suburb of **Castlecrag** ⑩, founded by Walter Burley Griffin, the American architect responsible for the design of Canberra.

On returning to the main body of the harbor, look to your right for the popular beach at Balmoral and **Middle Head** ⑪, part of Sydney Harbour National Park and the site of mid-19th-century

sydney harbour

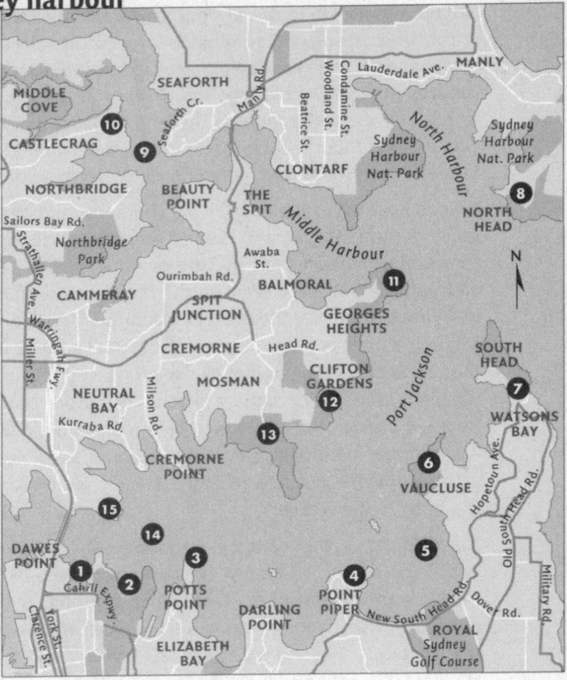

Castlecrag, 10
Chowder Bay, 12
Farm Cove, 2
Fort Denison, 14
Garden Island, 3
Kirribilli, 15
Middle Harbour, 9
Middle Head, 11
Point Piper, 4
Quarantine Station, 8
Rose Bay, 5
Sydney Cove, 1
Taronga Zoo, 13
Vaucluse, 6
Watsons Bay, 7

cannons and fortifications. During that period, Sydney Harbour became a regular port of call for American whaling ships, whose crews were responsible for the name of nearby **Chowder Bay** ⑫. Sailing deeper into the harbor, the vessel passes **Taronga Zoo** ⑬, where you might catch a glimpse of some of the animals through the foliage.

The vessel now heads back toward Harbour Bridge, passing the tiny island of **Fort Denison** ⑭, Sydney's most prominent fortification. On the point at **Kirribilli** ⑮, almost opposite the Opera House, you will catch glimpses of two colonial-style houses: the official Sydney residences of the governor-general and prime minister, who are otherwise based in Canberra. Still on the north side, but west of Harbour Bridge, lies Luna Park, Sydney's defunct amusement park.

From the north side of the harbor, the vessel crosses back to Circular Quay, where the tour ends.

TIMING

This scenic cruise, aboard one of the State Transit Authority ferries, takes 2½ hours and operates year-round. Refreshments are available on the boat's lower deck. For the best views, begin the voyage on the right side of the vessel.

Sights to See

❿ **CASTLECRAG.** This Middle Harbour suburb was founded by Walter Burley Griffin, an associate of Frank Lloyd Wright, after he designed Canberra. In 1924, after working on the national capital and in Melbourne, the American architect moved to Sydney and built a number of houses that are notable for their harmony with the surrounding bushland. About eight of his houses survive, although none are visible from the harbor.

⓬ **CHOWDER BAY.** In the 19th century, American whalers anchored here and made shellfish soup from the oysters that they collected from the rocks—and which gave the bay its name. The bay's location is identifiable by a cluster of wooden buildings at water's edge and twin oil-storage tanks.

❷ **FARM COVE.** Now the location of the **Royal Botanic Garden** (☞ Sights to See *in* The Opera House, the RBG, and the Domain North, *below*), the shore of this bay was where the first, unsuccessful attempts were made to establish gardens to feed the convict settlers. The long seawall was constructed from the 1840s onward to enclose the previously swampy foreshore.

⓮ **FORT DENISON.** For a brief time in the early days of the colony, convicts who committed petty offenses were kept on this harbor island. It was progressively fortified from 1841, when it was also decided to strengthen the existing defenses at Dawes Point Battery, under the Harbour Bridge. Work was abandoned when cash ran out and not completed until 1857, when fears of Russian expansion in the Pacific spurred further fortification. Today, the firing of the fort's cannon signals not an imminent invasion, but merely the hour—one o'clock. The National Parks and Wildlife Service runs two-hour-long tours to Fort Denison. Tours depart from Cadman's Cottage, 110 George Street, the Rocks. *Sydney Harbour, tel. 02/9247–5033.*

❸ **GARDEN ISLAND.** During the 1941–45 War of the Pacific, Australia's largest naval base and dockyard was a frontline port for Allied ships. On the night of May 31, 1942, this battle fleet was the target of three Japanese midget submarines that were launched from a mother submarine at sea. Two of the three penetrated the antisubmarine net that had been laid across the harbor and one sank the HMAS *Kuttabul*, a ferry being used as a naval depot ship, with a loss of 21 lives. Despite the ensuing chaos, two of the midget submarines were confirmed sunk.

Garden Island isn't open to the public, but the naval base may eventually be relocated outside Sydney, and there are plans to transform this prime harborside location into a recreational area.

15 **KIRRIBILLI.** Residents of this attractive suburb opposite the city and Opera House have million-dollar views, an excellent little theater, and two of Sydney's most important mansions. The more modest of the two is **Kirribilli House,** which is the official Sydney home of the prime minister and not open to the public. Next door and far more prominent is **Admiralty House**—the Sydney residence of the governor-general, the Queen's representative in Australia. This impressive residence is occasionally open for inspection. *Carabella St. and Kirribilli Ave. tel. 02/9955–4095.*

9 **MIDDLE HARBOUR.** Except for the sight of yachts moored in the sandy coves, the upper reaches of Middle Harbour are exactly as they were when the first Europeans set eyes on Port Jackson, just over 200 years ago. This area of bush- and parkland also has tranquil, desirable residential suburbs that are only a short drive from the city. Many of the houses here on the northern side of the harbor are set back from the waterline behind bushland. By the time these were built, planning authorities no longer allowed direct water frontage.

11 **MIDDLE HEAD.** Despite its benign appearance now, Sydney Harbour once bristled with armaments. In the middle of the last century, faced with expansionist European powers hungry for new colonies, artillery positions were erected on the headlands to guard harbor approaches. At Middle Head you can still see the rectangular gun emplacements set into the cliff face.

4 **POINT PIPER.** Many of this exclusive harborside suburb's magnificent dwellings are home to Sydney's rich and famous. Tom Cruise and Nicole Kidman purchased a home here in 1998, and waterfront mansions change hands for close to $20 million.

8 QUARANTINE STATION. From the 1830s onward ship passengers who arrived with contagious diseases were isolated on this outpost in the shadow of North Head until pronounced free of illness. Among the last to be quartered here were the victims of Cyclone Tracy, which devastated Darwin in 1974. Ten years later, after its brief use as a staging post for a group of Vietnamese orphans, the Quarantine Station was closed, its grim purpose finally brought to an end by modern medicine. You can take a 90-minute guided tour of the station with a ranger from the National Parks and Wildlife Service, caretakers of the site. Another interesting option is a three-hour nocturnal Ghost Tour. The station reputedly has its fair share of ghosts. The tour includes supper, and reservations are essential. The basic tour departs from Manly Wharf and the Ghost Tour departs from the visitor center at the Quarantine Station. Catch a ferry to Manly from Circular Quay and then take a taxi from Manly Wharf. *North Head, Manly, tel. 02/9977–6229.* $10 *basic tour, $17–$20 Ghost Tour. Basic tour Mon., Wed., and Fri. at 1:10; Ghost Tour Wed., Fri., and weekends at approximately* 8.

5 ROSE BAY. This large bay was once a base for the Qantas flying boats that provided the only passenger air service between Australia and America and Europe. The last flying boat departed Rose Bay in the 1960s, but the "airstrip" is still used by float planes on scenic flights connecting Sydney with the Hawkesbury River and the Central Coast.

1 SYDNEY COVE. Enclosed by Bennelong Point and the Sydney Opera House to the east and Circular Quay West and the Rocks to the west, the cove was named after Lord Sydney, the British Home Secretary at the time the colony was founded. The settlement itself was to be known as New Albion, but the name never caught on. Instead the city took its name from this tiny bay.

★ **13 TARONGA ZOO.** In a natural bush setting on the northern shore of the harbor, Sydney's zoo has an especially extensive collection of Australian fauna, including everybody's favorite marsupial the koala. The zoo has gone to great effort to create spacious enclosures that closely simulate natural habitats. It is set on a hillside, and a complete tour can be tiring, so you may want to pick up the free map at the entrance gate that outlines a less strenuous route. Children's strollers are provided free of charge, but they are rather basic.

The easiest way to get to the zoo from the city is by ferry. From Taronga Wharf a bus or the cable car will take you up the hill to the main entrance. The ZooPass, a combined ferry-zoo ticket, is available at Circular Quay. *Bradleys Head Rd., Mosman, tel. 02/9969–2777. $16. Daily 9–5. www.zoo.nsw.gov.au*

❻ **VAUCLUSE.** This is one of the most attractive harbor suburbs, and its palatial homes offer a glimpse of Sydney's high society. The small beaches at Nielsen Park and Parsley Bay offer safe swimming and are packed with families in summer.

A large part of this area once belonged to the estate of **Vaucluse House,** one of Sydney's most illustrious remaining historic mansions. Most of the Gothic Revival building was constructed in the 1830s for William Charles Wentworth, the "Father of the Australian Constitution," and his family. The 15-room house is furnished in period style, and its delightful gardens are managed by the Historic Houses Trust and open to the public. There are also famous old-style tearooms on the grounds. You can get to the house on the Bondi & Bay Explorer bus. *Wentworth Rd., Vaucluse, tel. 02/9388–7922. $6. Tues.–Sun. 10–4:30. www.hht.nsw.gov.au/MUSEUMS/vh.html*

❼ **WATSONS BAY.** Established as a military base and fishing settlement in the colony's early years, Watsons Bay is a charming suburb that has held on to its rare village atmosphere. Camp Cove, the main beach here, is of some historical importance: It was intended that the convicts who were to be Australia's first settlers would establish a community at Botany Bay, which had been explored by Captain Cook in 1770. However, as Captain Phillip found when he arrived 18 years later, the lack of freshwater at that site made settlement impossible. After a few days, he set off to explore Port Jackson, which had been named but not visited by Cook. Phillip rounded the Heads and landed on a beach that he named Camp Cove. The walkway that runs along the top of The Gap, the sheer cliffs at the southern approach to Port Jackson, commands a spectacular view of the surging sea far below.

THE ROCKS AND SYDNEY HARBOUR BRIDGE

The Rocks is the birthplace not just of Sydney but of modern Australia. It was here that the 11 ships of the First Fleet dropped anchor in 1788, and this stubby peninsula enclosing the western side of Sydney Cove became known simply as the Rocks.

The first crude wooden huts erected by the convicts were followed by simple houses made from mud bricks cemented together by a mixture of sheep's wool and mud. The rain soon washed this rough mortar away, and no buildings in the Rocks survive from the earliest period of convict settlement. Most of the architecture dates from the Victorian era, by which time Sydney had become a thriving port. Warehouses lining the waterfront were backed by a row of tradesmen's shops, banks, and taverns, and above them, ascending Observatory Hill, rose a tangled mass of alleyways lined with the cottages of seamen and wharf laborers. By the late 1800s all who could afford to had moved out of the area, and it was widely regarded as a rough, tough, squalid part of town. As late as 1900 bubonic plague swept through the Rocks, prompting the government to offer a bounty for dead rats in an effort to exterminate their disease-carrying fleas.

The character of the Rocks area changed considerably when the Sydney Harbour Bridge was built during the 1920s and '30s, when many old houses, and even entire streets, were demolished to make room for the bridge's southern approach route. The bridge took almost nine years to build and replaced the ferries that once carried passengers and freight across the harbor.

It is only since the 1980s that the Rocks has become appreciated for its historic significance and extensive restoration has transformed the area. Here you can see the evolution of a society almost from its inception to the present, and yet the Rocks is anything but a stuffy tutorial. History stands side by side with shops, outdoor cafés, and some excellent museums.

A Good Walk

Begin at **Circular Quay,** the lively waterfront area where Sydney's ferry, bus, and train systems converge. Follow the quay toward Harbour Bridge and, as you round the curve, turn left and walk about 20 paces into First Fleet Park. The map on the platform in front of you describes the colony of 1808. The **Tank Stream** entered Sydney Cove at this very spot. This tiny watercourse brought the colony its freshwater, the necessity that decided the location of the first European settlement on Australian soil.

Return to the waterfront and take the paved walkway toward Harbour Bridge. The massive art deco–style building to your left is the **Museum of Contemporary Art** ⑯, which is devoted to painting, sculpture, film, video, and kinetic art made during the past 20 years.

Continue on this walkway around **Circular Quay West,** and when you reach the fig trees in the circular bed, look left. The bronze statue beneath the trees is the figure of **William Bligh** ⑰ of HMAV *Bounty* fame. To the right is a two-story, cream-color stone house. This is **Cadman's Cottage** ⑱. Built in 1816, it is the oldest surviving house in the city of Sydney. The large modern building ahead of you on the waterfront is the **Overseas Passenger Terminal** ⑲, the main mooring for passenger liners in Sydney.

the rocks and harbour bridge

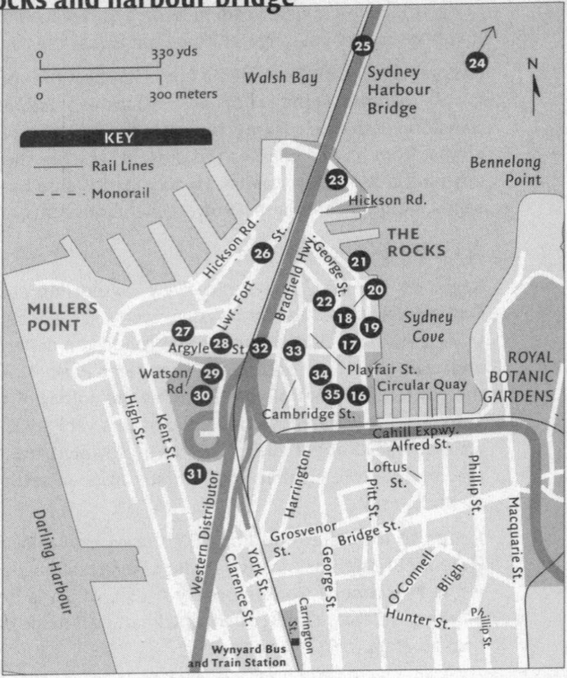

Argyle Cut, 32
Argyle Place, 27
Argyle Stores, 33
William Bligh Statue, 17
Cadman's Cottage, 18
Campbells Cove, 21
Dawes Point Park, 23
S. H. Ervin Gallery, 31
Fort Denison, 24
Holy Trinity Church, 28
Lower Fort Street, 26
Museum of Contemporary Art, 16
Nurses Walk, 35
Observatory Hill, 29
Overseas Passenger Terminal, 19
Suez Canal, 34
Sydney Harbour Bridge, 25
Sydney Observatory, 30
Sydney Visitors Information Centre, 20
Westpac Banking Museum, 22

Have a look inside Cadman's Cottage and then climb the stairs leading to George Street. Note the original gas street lamp at the top of these steps. Turn right and immediately on the right is the **Sydney Visitors Information Centre** ⑳, which has a bookshop and an information counter that can provide you with useful leaflets about the city.

After leaving the Information Centre, turn right past the redbrick facade of the Australian Steam Navigation Company. Continue down the hill and steps to **Campbells Cove** ㉑ and its warehouses. This carefully restored precinct contains numerous restaurants and cafés and is a great spot for harbor-watching and a drink or meal.

Walk back up the steps beside the warehouses and cross to **Upper George Street,** lined with restored 19th-century buildings. Across the road is **Atherden Street,** Sydney's shortest street. Note the small garden of staghorn ferns that has been painstakingly cultivated on tiny rock ledges at the end of this street. Just behind the Westpac Bank on the corner of George and Playfair streets is the **Westpac Banking Museum** ㉒, which has an exhibition dedicated to the history of the Olympic Games.

Continue up George Street toward the Sydney Harbour Bridge until you are directly beneath the bridge's massive girders. Note the iron green cubicle standing on the landward side of George Street. Modeled on the Parisian pissoir gentlemen's toilets such as this one were fairly common at the turn of the century, but they have since been replaced by the more discreet brick constructions. A modern toilet stands behind this sole survivor.

Walk under the bridge to **Dawes Point Park** ㉓ for excellent views of the harbor, including the Opera House and the small island of **Fort Denison** ㉔. This park also provides an unusual perspective on the **Sydney Harbour Bridge** ㉕—an unmistakable symbol of the city, and one of the world's widest long-span bridges.

Turn your back on the harbor and walk up **Lower Fort Street** ㉖, which runs to the right of the Harbour View Hotel. Continue up to the corner of Windmill Street, where you'll find the wedge-shaped **Hero of Waterloo,** one of the oldest pubs in the city.

Lower Fort Street ends at **Argyle Place** ㉗, built by Governor Macquarie and named after his home county in Scotland. The houses and other buildings here in the minisuburb of Millers Point are worth an inspection—particularly **Holy Trinity Church** ㉘ on the left-hand side and the **Lord Nelson Hotel** beyond the "village" green.

Argyle Place is dominated by **Observatory Hill** ㉙, the site of the colony's first windmill and, later, a signal station. If you have the energy to climb the steps that lead to the hill, you will reach a park shaded by giant Moreton Bay fig trees, where you will be rewarded with one of the finest views in Sydney. On top of the hill is the **Sydney Observatory** ㉚, now a museum of astronomy. You can also follow the path behind the Observatory to the National Trust Centre and the **S. H. Ervin Gallery** ㉛, which mounts changing exhibitions with Australian themes.

Leave Argyle Place and walk down **Argyle Street** into the dark tunnel of the **Argyle Cut** ㉜. On the lower side of the cut and to the left, the **Argyle Stairs** lead up through an archway. Don't take these steps unless you intend to tackle several flights of stairs that lead to the Harbour Bridge and into the **South East Pylon** for a dizzying view of the Opera House and the city. To get to the Sydney Harbour Bridge walkway from the top of the stairs, cross the road, walk left for 20 yards, and then follow the signs to the walkway and pylon. You should allow at least 1½ hours for this detour.

The walk resumes at the foot of the steps on Argyle Street. Continue down the street and turn left under the archway inscribed with the words **Argyle Stores** ㉝. The old warehouses around this courtyard have been converted to upmarket fashion shops and galleries. Leave the Argyle Stores and cross onto Harrington Street.

The **Gumnut Café** on the left-hand side of this street is a good place for a refreshment stop. Ten yards beyond the café is the **Suez Canal** ㉞, a narrow lane that runs down the incline toward George Street. Turn right at **Nurses Walk** ㉟, another of the area's historic and atmospheric back streets, then left into Surgeons Court and left again onto George Street. On the left is the handsome sandstone facade of the former **Rocks Police Station,** now a crafts gallery. From this point, Circular Quay is only a short walk away.

TIMING

The attractions of the Rocks are many, so to walk this route—even without lingering in museums or galleries or walking up to the Sydney Harbour Bridge—you should allow about a half day. If you spend a reasonable amount of time in the Museum of Contemporary Art, Sydney Observatory, and the S. H. Ervin Gallery, a full day is required.

The area is often very crowded on weekends, when the Rocks Market on George Street presents a serious distraction from sightseeing. The Rocks is also packed with interesting shops, so be forewarned that your time can rapidly disappear.

Sights to See

㉜ **ARGYLE CUT.** Argyle Street links Argyle Place with George Street, and the thoroughfare is dominated by the Argyle Cut and its massive walls. In the days before the cut was made, the sandstone ridge here was a major barrier to traffic crossing between Circular Quay and Millers Point. In 1843, convict work gangs hacked at the sandstone with hand tools for 2½ years before the project was abandoned due to lack of progress. Work restarted in 1857, when drills, explosives, and paid labor completed the job. The **Argyle Stairs** lead off this street up to the Sydney Harbour Bridge walkway, and a spectacular view from the South East Pylon (☞ Sydney Harbour Bridge, *below*).

27 **ARGYLE PLACE.** Unusual for Sydney, this charming enclave in the suburb of Millers Point has all the traditional requirements of an English green: a pub at one end, church at the other, and grass in between. Argyle Place is lined with 19th-century houses and cottages on its northern side and overlooked by Observatory Hill to the south.

NEED A BREAK? While in the west end of Argyle Place, consider the liquid temptations of the **Lord Nelson,** Sydney's oldest hotel, which has been licensed to serve alcohol since 1842. The sandstone pub has its own brewery on the premises. One of its specialties is Quayle Ale, named after the U.S. vice president who "sank a schooner" here during his 1989 visit to Australia. *19 Kent St., Millers Point, tel. 02/9251–4044.*

33 **ARGYLE STORES.** These solid sandstone warehouses date from the late 1820s and now house chic gift and souvenir shops, clothes boutiques, and cafés. *Argyle St. opposite Harrington St.*

17 **WILLIAM BLIGH STATUE.** Yes, this is the infamous captain—cursed both at sea and on land. After his incident on the *Bounty*, Bligh became governor of New South Wales in 1806. Two years later he faced his second mutiny. Bligh had made himself unpopular with the soldiers of the New South Wales Corps, commonly known as the Rum Corps, who were the real power in the colony. When he threatened to end their lucrative liquor trade monopoly, he was imprisoned in an incident known as the Rum Rebellion. He spent the next two years as a captive until his successor, Lachlan Macquarie, arrived. Ironically, the statue's gaze frequently rests on HMAV *Bounty*, a replica of Bligh's ship, as it sails around the harbor on daily sightseeing cruises.

18 **CADMAN'S COTTAGE.** Although of modest proportions, the city's oldest building has an interesting history. John Cadman was a convict who was sentenced for life to New South Wales for stealing a horse. He later became superintendent of government boats, a position that entitled him to live in the upper story of this house. The water once lapped almost at Cadman's doorstep, and the original seawall still stands at the front of the house. The small extension on the side of the cottage was built to lock up the oars of Cadman's boats, since oars would have been a necessity for any convict attempting to escape by sea. The upper floor of Cadman's Cottage now contains a National Parks and Wildlife Service bookshop and information center for Sydney Harbour National Park. *110 George St., tel. 02/9247–8861. Mon. 10–3, Tues.–Fri. 9–4:30, weekends 11–4.*

21 **CAMPBELLS COVE.** Robert Campbell was a Scottish merchant who is sometimes referred to as the "father of Australian commerce." Campbell broke the stranglehold that the British East India Company exercised over seal and whale products, which were New South Wales's only exports in those early days. The cove's atmospheric sandstone **Campbells Storehouse,** built from 1838 onward, now serves as a home for waterside restaurants. The pulleys that were used to hoist cargoes still hang on the upper level of the warehouses.

The cove is also the mooring for Sydney's fully operational tall ships—including the HMAV *Bounty*, an authentic replica of the original 18th-century vessel—which offer theme cruises around the harbor (☞ Practical Information).

23 **DAWES POINT PARK.** Named after William Dawes, a First Fleet marine and astronomer who established the colony's first basic observatory nearby in 1788, this was also once the site of a fortification known as Dawes Battery. The cannon on the hillside pointing toward the Opera House came from the ships of the First Fleet. The park provides wonderful views of the harbor, Fort Denison, and the Harbour Bridge.

31 **S. H. ERVIN GALLERY.** Housed in the impressive National Trust Centre just behind Observatory Hill, this gallery concentrates on Australian art and architecture from a historical perspective. The changing exhibitions are of a consistently high standard and have shown the work of such well-known Australian artists as Lloyd Rees, Sidney Nolan, Hans Heysen, and Russell Drysdale. The gallery has a bookshop, and there is a very good National Trust gift shop next door. *National Trust Centre, Observatory Hill, Watson Rd., Millers Point, tel. 02/9258–0123. $5. Tues.–Fri. 11–5, weekends noon–5.*

HARRINGTON STREET AREA. The small precinct around this street forms one of the Rocks's most interesting areas. Many old cottages, houses, and even warehouses here have been converted to hotel accommodations, and there are some fascinating lanes and alleyways to explore. ☞ **Nurses Walk** and ☞ **Suez Canal** are among them.

28 **HOLY TRINITY CHURCH.** Every morning redcoats would march to this 1840 Argyle Place church from Dawes Point Battery, and it became commonly known as the Garrison Church. As the regimental plaques and colors around the walls testify, the church still retains a close association with the military. The tattered ensign on the left wall was carried into battle by Australian troops during the Boer War, in which many Australians enlisted to help Great Britain in its war with South Africans of Dutch ancestry. *Argyle Pl., Millers Point, tel. 02/9247–1268. Daily, generally 9–5, but times vary.*

26 **LOWER FORT STREET.** At one time the handsome Georgian houses along this street, originally a rough track leading from the Dawes Point Battery to Observatory Hill, were among the best addresses in Sydney. Elaborate wrought-iron lacework still graces many of the facades.

Hero of Waterloo, which dates from 1844, is Sydney's second-oldest hotel. Gold fever struck the colony during the middle of the 19th century, and it was not uncommon for an entire ship's crew to desert and head for the goldfields as soon as the ship reached Sydney. Captains often resorted to skulduggery to recruit a new crew, and legend has it that many a lad who drank with a generous sea captain in the Hero would wake the next morning on a heaving deck, already out of sight of land. *81 Lower Fort St., tel. 02/9252–4553. Daily* 10 AM–11 PM.

16 **MUSEUM OF CONTEMPORARY ART.** Andy Warhol, Roy Lichtenstein, Cindy Sherman, and local artists Juan Devila, Maria Kozic, and Imants Tillers are just some of the well-known names whose works hang in this ponderous art-deco building on Circular Quay West. The MCA houses one of Australia's most important collections of modern art, and its special exhibitions are as worthwhile as the permanent collection. The museum's café, with outdoor seating beside the harbor, is pleasant for breakfast and lunch. *Circular Quay W, tel. 02/9252–4033. $9. Daily 10–6. www.mca.com.au*

35 **NURSES WALK.** Cutting across the area of the colony's first hospital, Nurses Walk bears its name out of the colony's earliest illnesses. Many of the 736 convicts who survived the voyage from Portsmouth, England, aboard the First Fleet's 11 ships arrived suffering from dysentery, smallpox, scurvy, and typhoid. A few days after he landed at Sydney Cove, Governor Phillip established a tent hospital to care for the worst cases.

Beyond Nurses Walk, the old **Rocks Police Station** on George Street dates from 1882 and now contains a variety of good crafts shops. Note the police truncheon thrust into the lion's mouth above the doorway, an architectural motif that appears on at least one other of Sydney's Victorian police stations.

NEED A BREAK? The **Gumnut Café** is more than just an ideal refreshment stop. In this second-oldest (1830) building in the Rocks—originally the residence of blacksmith William Reynolds—a painless history lesson comes with a delicious lunch. The restaurant tucked away in this sandstone cottage serves tasty salads, pasta dishes, and cakes. The best tables are at the back in the shady garden. The Gumnut has a devoted clientele, and reservations are necessary at lunchtime. If you're staying in the area, breakfast in the courtyard is a great start to the day. Prices are moderate. *28 Harrington St., tel. 02/9247–9591.*

---

29 **OBSERVATORY HILL.** The city's highest point at 145 ft, this was known originally as Windmill Hill because the first windmill in the colony once stood here. Soon after it was built, however, the canvas sails were stolen, the machinery was damaged in a storm, and the foundations cracked. Before it was 10 years old, the mill was useless. Several other windmills were erected in the area, however, and this part of the Rocks is still known as Millers Point. In 1848 the signal station at the top of the hill was built. This later became an astronomical observatory, and Windmill Hill changed its name to Observatory Hill. Until 1982 the metal ball on the tower of the observatory was cranked up the mast every afternoon and dropped at precisely 1:00 so ship captains could set their chronometers.

19 **OVERSEAS PASSENGER TERMINAL.** Busy **Circular Quay West** is dominated by the structure and dock of this maritime station, where ships often call into Sydney as part of their cruise itineraries. There are a couple of excellent waterfront restaurants at the terminal's northern end, and it's worth taking the escalator to the upper deck for a good view of the harbor and Opera House.

34 **SUEZ CANAL.** This narrow alley acquired its name before drains were installed, when rainwater would pour down its funnel-like passageway and gush across George Street. It was a haunt of the notorious Rocks gangs of the late 19th century, when robbery and other crimes were rife in the area.

25 **SYDNEY HARBOUR BRIDGE.** Known affectionately by Sydneysiders as the "old coat hanger," the Harbour Bridge was

a monumental engineering feat when it was completed in 1932. The roadway is supported by the arch above, not by the massive stone pylons, which were added for aesthetic rather than structural reasons. The 1,650-ft-long bridge is 160 ft wide and contains two sets of railway tracks, eight road lanes, a bikeway, and a footpath. Actor Paul Hogan worked for several years as a rigger on the bridge, long before he tamed the world's wildlife and lowlifes as the star of the film *Crocodile Dundee.*

There are two ways to experience the bridge and its spectacular views. The first, and less expensive, is to follow the walkway from its access point near the **Argyle Stairs** (☞ Argyle Cut, *above*) to the **South East Pylon.** This structure houses a display on the bridge's construction, and you can climb the 200 steps to the lookout and its unbeatable harbor panorama. *S. East Pylon, Sydney Harbour Bridge, tel. 02/9247–3408. $2. Daily 10–5.*

Another more expensive option is the BridgeClimb tour, which takes you on a guided walking tour to the very top of the Harbour Bridge.

30 **SYDNEY OBSERVATORY.** This structure on top of Observatory Hill is now a museum of astronomy. The Observatory features a number of hands-on displays, including constellation charts, talking computers, and games designed to illustrate principles of astronomy. During evening observatory shows, you'll have a close-up view of such wonders as the rings of Saturn, the moons of Jupiter, distant galaxies, and the enormous multicolored clouds of gas known as nebulae. Reservations are required for the show. *Observatory Hill, Watson Rd., Millers Point, tel. 02/9217–0485. Free; evening show $10. Observatory daily 10–5; show Nov.–Mar., Thurs.–Tues. at 8:30; Apr.–Oct., Thurs.–Tues. at 6:15 and 8:15.*

20 **SYDNEY VISITORS INFORMATION CENTRE.** Once a hotel that provided inexpensive accommodations for mariners, this building now offers insight into the history of the Rocks, with displays of

artifacts and a short video. Staff can answer questions about the area and make travel bookings, and the informative Rocks Walking Tours depart from here. The building also contains a couple of good places to eat: the very popular Sailor's Thai (☞ Rocks and Circular Quay *in* Eating Out) restaurant and its less expensive canteen. *106 George St., tel. 02/9255–1788. Mar.–Oct., daily 9–5; Nov.–Feb., daily 9–6.*

UPPER GEORGE STREET. The restored warehouses and Victorian terrace houses that line this part of George Street make this a charming section of the Rocks. The covered Rocks Market is held here on weekends (☞ Flea Markets *in* Shopping).

22 **WESTPAC BANKING MUSEUM.** On a lane off George Street, the museum displays a collection of coins from the earliest days of the colony of New South Wales. *6–8 Playfair St., tel. 02/9247–9755. Weekdays 9–5, weekends 10–4.*

MACQUARIE STREET AND THE DOMAIN SOUTH

This walk will introduce you to two of the most remarkable figures in Australian history: Governor Lachlan Macquarie and his government architect, Francis Greenway. Descended from Scottish clan chieftains, Macquarie was an accomplished soldier and a man of vision, the first governor to foresee a role for New South Wales as a free society rather than an open prison. Macquarie laid the foundations for that society by establishing a plan for the city, constructing significant public buildings, and advocating that reformed convicts be readmitted to society. Francis Greenway was himself a former prisoner.

Macquarie's policies may seem perfectly reasonable today, but in the early 19th century they marked him as a radical. When his vision of a free society threatened to blur distinctions between soldiers, settlers, and convicts, Macquarie was forced to resign. He was later buried on his Scottish estate, his gravestone inscribed with the words "the Father of Australia."

Macquarie's grand plans for the construction of Sydney might have come to nothing were it not for Francis Greenway. The governor had been continually frustrated by his masters in the Colonial Office in London, who saw no need for an architect in a penal colony. Then, in 1814, fate delivered Greenway into his hands. Greenway had trained as an architect in England, where he was convicted of forgery and sentenced to 14 years in New South Wales. Macquarie seized this opportunity, gave Greenway a ticket of leave that allowed him to work outside the convict system, and set him to work transforming Sydney.

For all his brilliance as an architect, Greenway was a difficult and temperamental man. When his patron Macquarie returned to England in 1822, Greenway quickly fell from favor and retired to his farm north of Sydney. Some years later he was charged with misappropriating this property, but he was able to produce a deed giving him title to the land. It is now believed that the signature on the title deed is a forgery. Greenway was depicted on one side of the old $10 notes, which went out of circulation early in the 1990s.

Only in Australia, perhaps, would a convicted forger be depicted on the currency.

A Good Walk

This historically based walk roughly follows the perimeter of the Royal Botanic Gardens and the Domain South. A shady park bench is never far away.

Begin at Circular Quay. Turn your back on the harbor and cross Alfred Street, which runs parallel to the waterfront. The most notable historic building along Alfred Street is the **Customs House** ㊱. When it was built in the late 1880s, the sandstone structure was surrounded by warehouses storing the fleeces that were the principal source of the colony's prosperity.

Walk up Loftus Street, which runs to the right of the Customs House. In Customs House Lane at the rear you can still see a pulley that was used to lower the wool bales to the dockyard from the top floor of Hinchcliff's Wool Stores.

Follow Loftus Street to the small triangular park on your right, **Macquarie Place** ㊲, which has a number of historical monuments. The southern side of the park is bordered by busy **Bridge Street,** lined with a number of grandiose Victorian buildings. Across Bridge Street, the **Lands Department** ㊳ is one of the finest examples of Victorian public architecture in Sydney. Walk up Bridge Street past the facade of the Department of Education. The **Museum of Sydney** ㊴ is on the next block. Built on the site of the first Government House, the museum chronicles the history of the city between 1788 and 1850.

Continue up Bridge Street to the corner of Macquarie Street. The figure on horseback about to gallop down Bridge Street is Edward VII, successor to Queen Victoria. The castellated building behind him is the **Sydney Conservatorium of Music** ㊵, originally built in 1819 as stables for Government House, which is screened by trees near the Opera House.

Your next stop is the lovely 1850s **History House** ㊶, headquarters of the Royal Australian Historical Society. It's just south of Bridge Street on **Macquarie Street**, Sydney's most elegant street. Opposite the History House are the **Garden Palace Gates** ㊷, an elegant wrought-iron entrance to the Royal Botanic Gardens. A little farther along Macquarie Street (Number 145) is the **Royal Australasian College of Physicians** ㊸. The patrician facade of this building gives some idea of the way Macquarie Street looked in the 1840s, when it was lined with the homes of the colonial elite.

The ponderous brown building ahead and to the left is the **State Library of New South Wales** ㊹. Cross the road toward this building, passing the **Light Horse Monument** and the **Shakespeare Memorial.** Australian cavalrymen fought with distinction in several Middle Eastern campaigns during World War I, and the former statue is dedicated to their horses, which were not allowed to return due to Australian quarantine regulations.

Continue along Macquarie Street toward the gates of **State Parliament House** ㊺, in the north wing of the former Rum Hospital. In a stroke of political genius, Governor Macquarie persuaded two merchants to build a hospital for convicts in return for an extremely lucrative three-year monopoly on the importation of rum.

The next building on the left is the Victorian-style **Sydney Hospital** ㊻, constructed to replace the central section of the Rum Hospital, which began to fall apart almost as soon as it was completed. Beyond the hospital is the **Sydney Mint** ㊼, originally the Rum Hospital's southern wing.

Next door is the **Hyde Park Barracks** ㊽. Before Macquarie arrived, convicts were left to roam freely at night, and there was little regard for the sanctity of life or property on the streets of Sydney after dark. As the new governor, Macquarie was determined to establish law and order, and he commissioned Greenway to design this building to house prisoners. Opposite Hyde Park Barracks is the 1970s high-rise **Law Court** building. This area is the heart of Sydney's legal district.

Cross Queens Square to the other side of the road, where the figure of Queen Victoria presides over Macquarie Street. To Victoria's left is another Greenway building, **St. James Church** ㊾, originally designed as a court of law.

Return to the other side of Macquarie and walk along College Street to **St. Mary's Cathedral** ㊿. This is Sydney's Roman Catholic church, whose design is based on Lincoln Cathedral in England. Note the pointed arches above the doors and flying buttresses (the arches that connect the side of the cathedral to supporting piers). Both are signatures of Gothic style.

At the rear of the cathedral, cross St. Mary's Road to Art Gallery Road. You are now in the parklands of **the Domain South** (51),

macquarie street and the domain

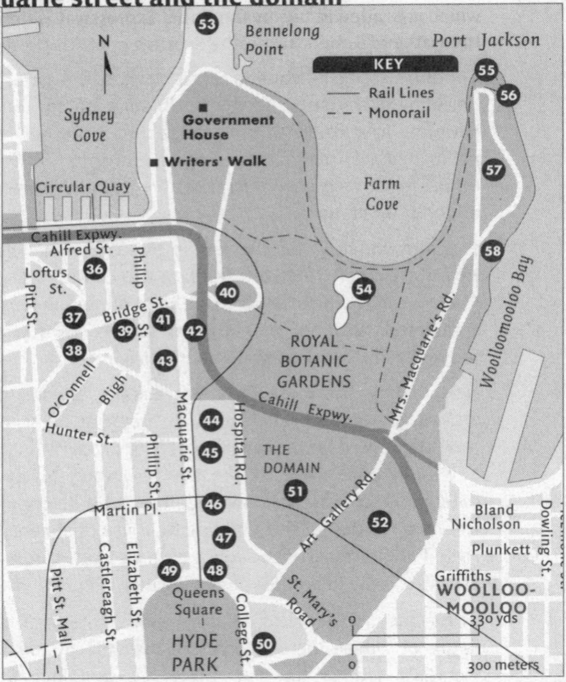

Andrew (Boy) Charlton Pool, 58
Art Gallery of New South Wales, 52
Customs House, 36
The Domain North, 57
The Domain South, 51
Garden Palace Gates, 42
History House, 41
Hyde Park Barracks, 48
Lands Department, 38
Macquarie Place, 37
Mrs. Macquarie's Chair, 56
Mrs. Macquarie's Point, 55
Museum of Sydney, 39
Royal Australasian College of Physicians, 43
Royal Botanic Gardens, 54
St. James Church, 49
St. Mary's Cathedral, 50
State Library of New South Wales, 44
State Parliament House, 45
Sydney Conservatorium of Music, 40
Sydney Hospital, 46
Sydney Mint, 47
Sydney Opera House, 53

which is divided in two by the Cahill Expressway. Continue past the statue of Robert Burns, the Scottish poet. The large trees on the left with enormous roots and drooping limbs are the widely planted Moreton Bay figs, which bear inedible fruit. Directly ahead is the **Art Gallery of New South Wales** (52), housed in a grand Victorian building with modern extensions. It contains the state's largest collection of artwork. From the Art Gallery, you can return to Macquarie Street by crossing the Domain or wandering for a half mile through the Royal Botanic Gardens. If you have an Explorer bus pass, you can catch the bus back to the city center from the front of the gallery.

TIMING

To walk the outlined itinerary should take no more than a morning or afternoon, even with stops to inspect the Museum of Sydney, Sydney Mint, Hyde Park Barracks, and the Art Gallery of New South Wales. Apart from the initial climb from Circular Quay to Macquarie Street, the terrain is flat and easy.

Sights to See

52 **ART GALLERY OF NEW SOUTH WALES.** This gallery permanently exhibits Aboriginal, Asian, and European art, as well as the work of some of the best-known Australian artists. A distinctly Australian style has evolved, from early painters who saw the country through European eyes to such painters as Russell Drysdale, whose strident colors and earthy realism give a very different impression of the Australian landscape.

The entrance level, where large windows frame spectacular views of the harbor, holds 20th-century art. Below, in the gallery's major extensions, the Yiribana Gallery displays one of the nation's most comprehensive collections of Aboriginal and Torres Strait Islander art. The bookshop on the ground floor has an offbeat collection of souvenirs. *Art Gallery Rd., the Domain, tel. 02/9225–1744. Free, special-exhibition fee varies. Daily 10–5. www.artgallery.nsw.gov.au*

36 **CUSTOMS HOUSE.** Close to the site where the British flag was raised on the First Fleet's arrival in 1788, this impressive 1840s–1890s building was in use until 1990 as the city's Customs House and later as offices. The building now houses the Centre for Contemporary Craft, a retail crafts gallery, and the Djamu Gallery, Australia's largest permanent exhibition of Aboriginal and Pacific Island artifacts. The standout in the clutch of restaurants and cafés in this newly sparkling historic structure is the rooftop Café Sydney, overlooking Sydney Cove. *Customs House Sq., Alfred St., Circular Quay, tel. 02/9265–2007.*

51 **THE DOMAIN SOUTH.** Laid out by Governor Macquarie in 1810 as his own personal "domain" and originally including what is now the Royal Botanic Gardens, this large area of parkland is a tranquil haven at the city's eastern edge. Used mainly by office workers for lunchtime recreation, the park is also the venue for free outdoor concerts during the Festival of Sydney in January.

42 **GARDEN PALACE GATES.** The gates are all that remains of the Garden Palace, a massive glass pavilion that was erected for the Sydney International Exhibition of 1879 and destroyed by fire three years later. On the arch above the gates is a depiction of the Garden Palace's dome. Stone pillars on either side of the gates are engraved with Australian wildflowers. *Macquarie St. between Bridge and Bent Sts.*

41 **HISTORY HOUSE.** You're welcome to visit the home of the Royal Australian Historical Society and its collection of books and other materials. Note the balconies and the Corinthian columns, all made from iron, which was just becoming popular when this building was constructed in 1872. *133 Macquarie St., tel. 02/9247–8001. Library $5. Weekdays 9:30–4:30.*

Macquarie Street is Sydney's most elegant boulevard. It was masterminded by Governor Macquarie, who, from 1810 until he was ousted in 1822, planned the transformation of the cart track leading to Sydney Cove into a stylish street of dwellings and government buildings. Fortunately, many of the 19th-century architectural delights here escaped demolition.

48 **HYDE PARK BARRACKS.** This 1819 building is considered Greenway's architectural masterpiece. Essentially a simple structure, its restrained classical lines are hallmarks of the Georgian era. The clock on the tower is the oldest functioning public timepiece in New South Wales. Today the Hyde Park Barracks houses "Convicts," an exhibition that explores the background to the banishment of prisoners to the island continent of Australia. A surprising number of relics from this period were preserved by rats, which carried away scraps of clothing for their nests beneath the floorboards. This bizarre detail is graphically illustrated in the foyer. A room on the top floor is strung with hammocks, exactly as it was when the building housed convicts. *Queens Sq., Macquarie St., tel. 02/9223–8922. $6. Daily 9:30–5.*

NEED A BREAK? On a sunny day, the courtyard tables of the **Hyde Park Barracks Café** provide one of the finest places in the city to enjoy an outdoor lunch. The café serves a selection of light, imaginative meals, salads, and open sandwiches, with a wine list including Australian vintages. Prices are moderate. *Queens Sq., Macquarie St., tel. 02/9223–1155.*

38 **LANDS DEPARTMENT.** The figures occupying the niches at the corners of this 1890 sandstone building are early Australian explorers and politicians. James Barnet's building stands among other fine Victorian structures in the neighborhood. *Bridge St., near the intersection of Macquarie Pl.*

37 **MACQUARIE PLACE.** This park, once a site of ceremonial and religious importance to Aboriginal people, contains a number of important monuments, including the obelisk formerly used as the point from which all distances from Sydney were measured. On a stone plinth at the bottom of the park is the anchor of HMS

Sirius, flagship of the First Fleet, which struck a reef and sank off Norfolk Island in 1790. The bronze statue of the gentleman with his hands on his hips represents Thomas Mort, who more than a century ago became the first person to ship refrigerated cargo. The implications of this shipment were enormous. Mutton suddenly became a valuable export commodity, and for most of the next century the Australian economy rode on sheep's backs.

Bridge Street runs alongside Macquarie Place. Formerly the site of the 1789 Government House and the colony's first bridge, this V-shaped street was named for the bridge that once crossed the Tank Stream. Today a number of grandiose Victorian architectural specimens line its sidewalks.

39 **MUSEUM OF SYDNEY.** Built on the site of the modest original Government House, this museum documents Sydney's early period of European colonization. One of the most interesting features is outside: the striking Edge of the Trees sculpture, with its 29 columns that "speak" and contain remnants of Aboriginal and early European inhabitation. Inside, Aboriginal culture, convict society, and the gradual transformation of the settlement at Sydney Cove are woven into the single most evocative portrayal of life in the early days of the country. The museum has a popular café and a shop that stocks unusual gifts and other items. *Bridge and Phillip Sts., tel. 02/9251–5988. $6. Daily 10–5. www.mos.nsw.gov.au*

Also near the intersection of Bridge Street and Phillip Street is an imposing pair of sandstone buildings. The historic **Treasury Building** is now part of the Hotel Inter-Continental. James Barnet's **Colonial Secretary's Office**—he also designed the Lands Department—is opposite. Note the buildings' similarities, right down to the figures in the corner niches.

43 **ROYAL AUSTRALASIAN COLLEGE OF PHYSICIANS.** Once the home of a wealthy Sydney family, the building now houses a different elite: the city's most eminent physicians. *Macquarie St. between Bridge and Bent Sts.*

49 **ST. JAMES CHURCH.** Begun in 1822, the Colonial Georgian–style St. James is Sydney's oldest surviving church, and another fine Francis Greenway design. Meant to be the colony's first law court, the building was half completed when Commissioner Bigge, who had been sent from England to investigate Macquarie's administration, ordered that the structure be converted into a church. Now lost among the skyscrapers, the church's tall spire once served as a landmark for ships entering the harbor.

Enter St. James through the door in the Doric portico. The interior walls of the church are covered with plaques commemorating Australian explorers and administrators. Inscriptions on the plaques testify to the hardships of those early days, when death either at sea or at the hands of Aborigines was a common fate. *Queens Sq., Macquarie St., tel. 02/9232–3022. Daily 9–5.*

50 **ST. MARY'S CATHEDRAL.** The first St. Mary's was built here in 1821, but the chapel was destroyed by fire, and work on the present cathedral began in 1868. The building isn't complete, though. Due to a shortage of funds, spires for the front towers were never added. St. Mary's has some particularly fine stained-glass windows and a terrazzo floor in the crypt, where exhibitions are often held. The cathedral's large rose window was imported from England.

At the front of the cathedral are statues of Cardinal Moran and Archbishop Kelly, two Irishmen who were prominent in the Roman Catholic Church in Australia. Due to the high proportion of Irish men and women in the convict population, the Roman Catholic Church was often the voice of the oppressed in 19th-century Sydney, where anti-Catholic feeling ran high among the Protestant rulers. Australia's first cardinal, Patrick Moran, was a powerful exponent of Catholic education and a diplomat who did much to heal the rift between the two faiths. By contrast, Michael Kelly, his successor as head of the church in Sydney, was excessively pious and politically inept; Kelly and Moran remained at odds until Moran's death in 1911. *College and*

Cathedral Sts., tel. 02/9220–0400. Tour free. Weekdays 6:30–6:30, Sat. 8–7:30, Sun. 6:30 AM–7:30 PM; tour Sun. at noon.

44 **STATE LIBRARY OF NEW SOUTH WALES.** This large complex is based around the Mitchell and Dixson libraries, which house the world's largest collection of Australiana. The general reference collection housed in the library's modern extension on Macquarie Street is generally of more interest, however. The extension has an excellent shop for books and gifts, a café, free films, and changing exhibitions with Australian historical and cultural themes in the upstairs gallery.

The foyer inside the heavy glass doors of the imposing 1910 Mitchell Wing contains one of the earliest maps of Australia, a copy in marble mosaic of a map made by Abel Tasman, the Dutch navigator. Tasman wasn't the first European to set eyes on the Australian coastline, but his voyages established that Australia was not the fabled Great South Land for which the Dutch had been searching. On his first voyage to Australia in 1642–43, Tasman sailed along the southern coast of Australia and discovered Tasmania, which he named Van Diemen's Land in honor of his patron, the governor of the Dutch East Indies. On his next voyage in 1644, Tasman explored much of the north coast of Australia. On the mosaic map the two ships of the first voyage are shown off the south coast in the Great Australian Bight. The ships of the second voyage are shown off the northwest coast. Marble for the map came from Wombeyan, about 160 km (100 mi) southwest of Sydney.

Beyond the map and through the glass doors is the vast reading room of the Mitchell Library, but you need a reader's ticket (establishing that you are pursuing legitimate research) to enter. You can, however, take a free escorted tour of the library's buildings. *Macquarie St., tel. 02/9230–1414. Weekdays 9–9, weekends 11–5; General Reference Library tour Tues.–Thurs. at 2:30; Mitchell Library tour Tues. and Thurs. at 11. www.slnsw.gov.au*

45 **STATE PARLIAMENT HOUSE.** This 1816 Rum Hospital building, with its simple facade and shady verandas, is a classic example of Australian colonial architecture. From 1829, two rooms of the old hospital were used for meetings of the executive and legislative councils, which had been set up to advise the governor. The functions of these advisory bodies grew until New South Wales became self-governing in the 1840s, at which time Parliament occupied the entire building. The Legislative Council Chamber—the upper house of the parliament, identifiable by its red color scheme—is a prefabricated cast-iron structure that was originally intended to be a church on the goldfields of Victoria.

State Parliament generally sits between mid-February and late May, and again between mid-September and late November. Visitors are welcome to the public gallery to watch the local version of the Westminster system of democracy in action. On weekdays, generally between 9:30 and 4, you can tour the building's public areas, which contain a number of portraits and paintings. You must make reservations. *Macquarie St., tel. 02/9230–2111. Weekdays, 9:30–4; hours vary when Parliament is in session.*

40 **SYDNEY CONSERVATORIUM OF MUSIC.** Once the governor's stables, this fortresslike Gothic Revival building presents a marked departure from Francis Greenway's normally simple and elegant designs. The cost of constructing the stables caused a storm among Governor Macquarie's superiors in London and eventually helped bring about the downfall of both Macquarie and his architect.

On an irregular basis, this establishment's talented students give free lunchtime (usually Wednesday and Friday) and evening concerts. Call for details. *Conservatorium Rd., off Macquarie St., tel. 02/9230–1222.*

46 **SYDNEY HOSPITAL.** Completed in 1894 as the replacement for the main Rum Hospital building, this institution offered an infinitely better medical option. By all accounts, admission to the Rum Hospital was only slightly preferable to death itself. Convict

nurses stole patients' food, and abler patients stole from the weaker. The kitchen sometimes doubled as a mortuary, and the kitchen table was occasionally used to perform operations. *Macquarie St. and Martin Pl.*

In front of the hospital is a bronze figure of a boar. This is *Il Porcellino*, a copy of a statue that stands in Florence, Italy. According to the inscription, if you make a donation in the coin box and rub the boar's nose, "you will be endowed with good luck." Sydney citizens seem to be a superstitious bunch because the boar's nose is very shiny indeed.

47 **SYDNEY MINT.** The south wing of Greenway's 1816 Rum Hospital became a branch of the Royal Mint after the 1850s Australian gold rushes, which lured thousands of gold miners from around the world. Previously a museum, the building is currently used as government offices. It also houses a small café, and storyboards inside illustrate the building's history. *Macquarie St.*

THE OPERA HOUSE, THE RBG, AND THE DOMAIN NORTH

Bordering Sydney Cove, Farm Cove, and Woolloomooloo Bay, this section of Sydney includes the iconic, symbolic Sydney Opera House, as well as extensive gardens and parkland that create a delightful harborside haven.

The colony's first farming attempt began here in 1788, and the botanical gardens were initiated in 1816. The most dramatic change to the area occurred in 1959, however, when ground was broken on the site for the Sydney Opera House at Bennelong Point. This promontory was originally a small island, then the site of 1819 Fort Macquarie, and later a tram depot that did little to enhance the cityscape.

A Good Walk

From Circular Quay, walk around Sydney Cove along Circular Quay East. This walkway is also known as **Writers' Walk.** Brass plaques embedded in the sidewalk commemorate prominent Australian writers, playwrights, and poets. The apartment buildings along the landward side of the street have some of the best views in Sydney, yet they caused enormous controversy when they were built in the late 1990s. One look and you'll see why the building closest to the Opera House is known to all as "The Toaster."

Ahead, on the Bennelong Point promontory, is the unmistakable **Sydney Opera House** ⑬. Its distinctive white tiled "sails" and prominent position make this the most widely recognized landmark of urban Australia. The Opera House has fueled controversy and debate among Australians, but whatever its detractors may say, the Opera House leaves no visitor unmoved.

The **Royal Botanic Gardens** (54) are behind the Opera House, combining with the rolling parkland of the Domain to form the eastern border of the city. You can either walk around the Farm Cove pathway or head inland to spend some time exploring the gardens, including a stop at **Government House,** before returning to the waterfront.

The pathway around the cove leads to a peninsula, **Mrs. Macquarie's Point** (55), in the northern part of the Domain. It is named for Elizabeth Macquarie, the governor's wife, who planned the road through the parkland. As you round the peninsula and turn toward the naval dockyard at Garden Island, notice the small bench carved into the rock with an inscription identifying it as **Mrs. Macquarie's Chair** (56).

Continue through **the Domain North** (57) on Mrs. Macquarie's Road to the **Andrew (Boy) Charlton Pool** (58), built over Woolloomooloo Bay. It's a great spot for a summer swim. From the pool there are good views of the Garden Island naval base and the suburb of Potts Point, across the bay.

This road eventually takes you to the southern part of the Domain. The once-continuous Domain is divided into north and south sections by the Cahill Expressway, which leads up to the Sydney Harbour Bridge and down into the **Sydney Harbour Tunnel.** The tunnel was completed in the early 1990s and has helped to alleviate traffic congestion on the bridge.

At the end of the walk, you can return to the city and Macquarie Street by reentering the botanical gardens through the Woolloomooloo Gate near the roadway over the Cahill Expressway.

TIMING

A walk around the Sydney Opera House, Royal Botanic Gardens, and the Domain North can easily be accomplished in a morning or afternoon. The walk is highly recommended on a warm summer evening. Allow more time if you wish to explore the gardens more thoroughly. These are delightful at any time of year, though they're especially beautiful in spring.

Sights to See

58 **ANDREW (BOY) CHARLTON POOL.** Named after one of Australia's famous swimmers, this Olympic-size saltwater pool is extremely popular with locals in summer. It's the perfect place to cool off if you're walking this route on a hot day. *The Domain North, tel. 02/9358–6686. $2. Oct.–Apr., weekdays 6 AM–7 PM, weekends 6:30–6.*

57 **THE DOMAIN NORTH.** The northern part of the Domain adjoins the Royal Botanic Gardens and extends from Mrs. Macquarie's Point to the Cahill Expressway. Surrounded by Farm Cove and Woolloomooloo Bay, this is a pleasant, harbor-fringed area of parkland that encompasses all sights mentioned in this section, excluding the Opera House on Bennelong Point.

56 **MRS. MACQUARIE'S CHAIR.** During the early 1800s, Elizabeth Macquarie often sat on the point in the Domain at the east side of Farm Cove, at the rock where a seat has been hewn in her name.

55 **MRS. MACQUARIE'S POINT.** With excellent views of the harbor and north shore, the point and its waterside lawns are a popular

place for picnics, especially on warm summer evenings when the sunset makes a spectacular backdrop to the Opera House and Harbour Bridge.

54 **ROYAL BOTANIC GARDENS.** Groves of palm trees, duck ponds, a cactus garden, a restaurant, greenhouses, and acres of lawns come together in Sydney's finest gardens, where the convicts of the First Fleet established a farm. Their early attempts at agriculture were disastrous, as the soil was poor and few of the convicts came from an agricultural background. For the first couple of years the prisoners and their guards existed on the verge of starvation. The colony was eventually saved by the arrival of a supply ship in 1790.

The gardens were founded in 1816 and greatly expanded during the 1830s. The wonderful collection of plants and trees are both native Australians and exotics from around the world, and garden highlights include the Sydney Tropical Centre, housed in the Pyramid and Arc glass houses, and the lush Sydney Fernery. The visitor center is worth a visit, as is the excellent Botanic Gardens Restaurant. The Gardens Shop has unusual souvenirs. Tours leave from the visitor center, near the Art Gallery of New South Wales. *The Domain North, tel. 02/9231–8125. Sydney Tropical Centre $5, tour free. Royal Botanic Gardens daily sunrise–sunset; Sydney Tropical Centre and Sydney Fernery daily 10–4; tour daily at 10:30. www.rbgsyd.gov.au*

Completed in 1843, the two-story, sandstone, Gothic Revival **Government House** served as the residence of the Governor of New South Wales—who represents the British crown in local matters—until the Labor Party Government handed it back to the public in 1996. The building was designed by the prominent English architect Edward Blore, who completed the plan without ever setting foot in Australia. The house's stenciled ceilings, which were repainted in the 1980s, are its most impressive feature. Paintings hanging on the walls bear the signatures of some of Australia's best-known artists, including Roberts,

Streeton, and Drysdale. You are free to wander on your own around Government House's gardens, which lie within the Royal Botanic Gardens, but you must join a guided tour to see the house's interior. *Royal Botanic Gardens, tel. 02/9931–5200. Free. House Fri.–Sun. 10–3; gardens daily 10–4.*

53 **SYDNEY OPERA HOUSE.** The Opera House had such a long and troubled construction process that it's no minor miracle the building exists at all. In 1954, the state premier appointed a committee to advise the government on the building of an opera house. The site chosen was Bennelong Point, which until that time was the site of a tram depot. The premier's committee launched a competition to find a suitable plan, and a total of 233 submissions came in from architects from all over the world. One of them was a young Dane named Joern Utzon.

His plan was brilliant, but it had all the markings of a monumental disaster. The structure was so narrow that stages would have minuscule wings, and the soaring "sails" that formed the walls and roof could not be built by existing technology.

Nonetheless, Utzon's dazzling, dramatic concept caught the judges' imagination, and construction of the giant podium began in 1958. From the start, the contractors faced a cost blowout, a problem that was to plague the Opera House throughout its construction. The building that was projected to cost $7 million and take four years to erect would eventually require $102 million and 15 years. Construction was financed by an intriguing scheme that appealed to Australian's fondness for gambling. Realizing that citizens might be hostile to the use of public funds for the controversial project, the state government raised the money through the Opera House Lottery. The payout was huge by the standards of the time: $100,000 for first prize. For almost a decade, Australians lined up to buy tickets, and the Opera House was built without depriving the state's hospitals or schools of a single cent.

Initially it was thought that the concrete exterior of the building would have to be cast in place, which would have meant building an enormous birdcage of scaffolding at even greater expense. Then, as he was peeling an orange one day, Utzon had a flash of inspiration. Why not construct the shells from segments of a single sphere? The concrete ribs forming the skeleton of the building could be prefabricated in just a few molds, hoisted into position, and joined together. These ribs are clearly visible inside the Opera House, especially in the foyers and staircases of the Concert Hall.

In 1966, Utzon resigned as Opera House architect and left Australia, embittered by his dealings with unions and the government. He has never returned to see his masterpiece. A team of young Australian architects carried on, completing the exterior one year later. Until that time, however, nobody had given much thought to the *interior*. The shells created awkward interior spaces, and conventional performance areas were simply not feasible. It is a tribute to the architectural team's ingenuity that the exterior of the building is matched by the aesthetically pleasing and acoustically sound theaters inside.

In September 1973 the Australian Opera performed *War and Peace* in the Opera Theatre. A month later, Queen Elizabeth II officially opened the building in a ceremony capped by an astonishing fireworks display. Nowadays, the controversies that raged around the building seem moot. Poised majestically on its peninsula, with Circular Quay and Harbour Bridge on one side and the Royal Botanic Gardens on the other, it has become a loved and potent national symbol.

The building is actually far more versatile than its name implies. In reality, it is an entertainment complex allowing a wide range of performances and activities: dance, drama, films, opera, and jazz. It also has four restaurants and cafés, and several bars that cater to the hordes of patrons. Guided one-hour tours of the Opera House depart at frequent intervals from the tour office, on the lower forecourt level, 9:15–4 on most days. All tours can be restricted or suspended due to performances or rehearsals. Call in advance. *Bennelong Point, tel. 02/9250–7111. Tour $12.90. www.soh.nsw.gov.au*

DARLING HARBOUR

Until the mid-1980s, this horseshoe-shape bay on the western edge of the city center was a wasteland of disused docks and railway yards. Then, in an explosive burst of activity, the whole area was redeveloped and opened in time for Australia's bicentennial in 1988. Now there's plenty to take in at the Darling Harbour complex: the National Maritime Museum, the large Harbourside shopping and dining center, the Sydney Aquarium, the Cockle Bay waterfront dining complex, and the gleaming Exhibition Centre, whose masts and spars recall the square riggers that once berthed here. At the harbor's center is a large park shaded by palm trees. The Panasonic IMAX Theatre and the Sega World indoor theme park stand at the harbor's periphery. The complex is laced together by a series of waterways and fountains.

The Powerhouse Museum is within easy walking distance, and immediately to the south are Chinatown and the Sydney Entertainment Centre. The Star City entertainment complex, with Star City Casino (☞ Nightlife *in* Nightlife and the Arts) as its centerpiece, is the newest addition to the area. It lies just to the west of Darling Harbour.

A Good Walk

Start at the Market Street end of Pitt Street Mall, Sydney's main pedestrian shopping precinct. Take the monorail—across Market Street and above ground level on the right-hand side of Pitt Street—from here to the next stop (Darling Park), passing the large Queen Victoria Building on your left. Get off at this stop and go down the steps and escalator. On your right is **Sydney**

Aquarium (59), the city's first-class fishbowl full of exotic creatures with fins, flippers, and scales.

From here, take the escalator back up to historic **Pyrmont Bridge** (60) and walk across to the **Australian National Maritime Museum** (61), the large white-roof building on your right. Documenting Australia's vital links with the ocean, the museum features everything from Aboriginal canoes to ships and surfboards.

After visiting the Maritime Museum you can explore the Harbourside center, a good place for a drink or a meal. Then walk through Darling Harbour, where you'll notice beside the elevated freeway a curved building with a checkerboard pattern. This is the **Panasonic IMAX Theatre** (62), the world's largest movie screen, featuring a series of stunning special-effect presentations. From the theater, cross under the elevated freeway and walk past the carousel. On your left is Sydney's first indoor theme park, **Sega World** (63), easily identified by the transparent blue cone on its roof.

The intriguing **Powerhouse Museum** (64) is a worthwhile detour from the amusements of Darling Harbour. Walk west to Merino Boulevard. Then continue south to William Henry Street and turn right. The museum is just south of the intersection of William Henry and Harris streets. Housed inside an old power station with extensive modern additions, this is by far the city's largest museum, with a vast collection from the Museum of Applied Arts and Sciences.

From the Powerhouse, walk back to William Henry Street and follow it east until it becomes Pier Street. Here you'll find the **Chinese Garden** (65).

You can return to the city center by monorail—follow signs to the Haymarket station—or take a short walk around the colorful streets, shops, markets, and restaurants of Chinatown, just south of the Chinese Garden.

sydney suburbs

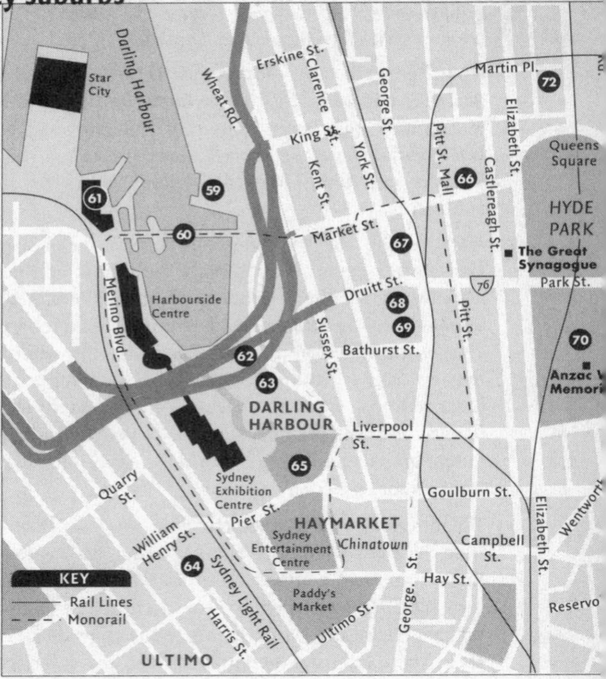

AMP Tower, 66
Arthur McElhone Reserve, 74
Australian National Maritime Museum, 61
Australian Museum, 71
Beare Park, 75
Chinese Garden, 65
Elizabeth Bay House, 73
Hyde Park, 70
Juniper Hall, 79
Martin Place, 72
Panasonic IMAX Theatre, 62
Powerhouse Museum, 64
Pyrmont Bridge, 60

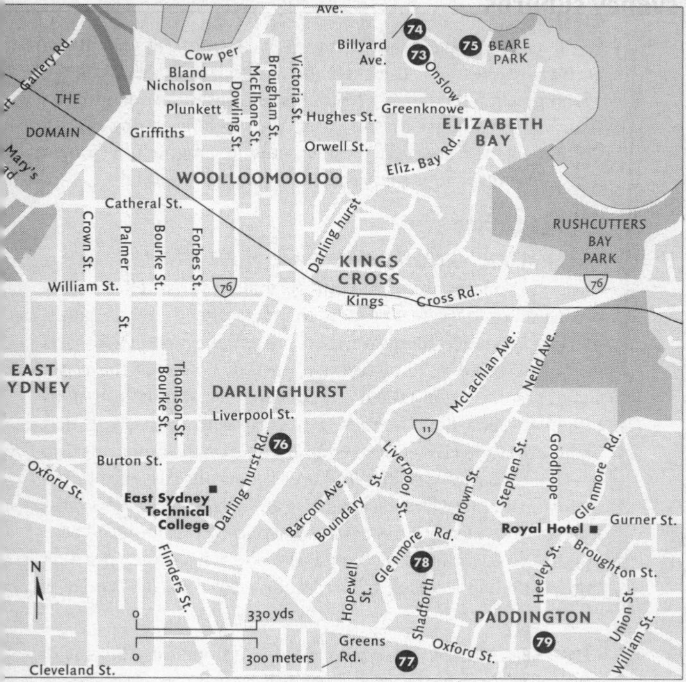

ueen Victoria
uilding, 67
Andrew's
athedral, 69
ega World, 63
adforth Street, 78
Sydney
Aquarium, 59
Sydney Jewish
Museum, 76
Sydney
Town Hall, 68
Victoria
Barracks, 77

TIMING

You'll need at least a half day to see the best of the area. If you aren't so interested in the museums, a good time to visit is in the evening, when the tall city buildings reflect the sunset and cast their magical images on the water. You might even pop over to Chinatown for dinner. Later, pubs, cafés, and nightclubs turn on lights and music for a party that lasts well past midnight.

Sights to See

61 **AUSTRALIAN NATIONAL MARITIME MUSEUM.** This soaring, futuristic building is divided into six galleries that tell the story of Australia and the sea. In addition to figureheads, model ships, and brassy nautical hardware, there are antique racing yachts and the jet-powered *Spirit of Australia*, current holder of the water speed record. Among the many spectacular exhibits is the fully rigged *Australia II*, the famous 12-m yacht with winged keel that finally broke the Newport Yacht Club's hold on the America's Cup in 1983. An outdoor section features numerous vessels moored at the museum's wharves, including HMAS *Vampire*, a World War II destroyer, a fishing boat that transported Vietnamese "boat people" to Australia in 1977, and a northern Australian pearling lugger. *Darling Harbour, tel. 02/9298–3777. $20. Daily 9:30–5. www.anmm.gov.au*

65 **CHINESE GARDEN.** The nation's long and enduring links with China—Chinese prospectors came to the Australian goldfields as far back as the 1850s—are symbolized by this tranquil walled enclave. Designed by Chinese landscape architects, the garden includes bridges, lakes, waterfalls, and Cantonese-style pavilions. This is the perfect spot for a break from sightseeing and Darling Harbour's crowds. *Darling Harbour, tel. 02/9281–6863. $3. Daily 9:30–5:30.*

62 **PANASONIC IMAX THEATRE.** Both in size and dramatic impact, this eight-story-tall movie screen is overwhelming. Inside, a series of one-hour presentations takes you on astonishing, wide-

angle voyages of discovery into space, to ancient Egypt, or to the summit of Mount Everest. *Darling Harbour, tel. 02/9281–3300. $15.00. Daily 10–10. www.imax.com.au*

64 **POWERHOUSE MUSEUM.** This extraordinary museum of applied arts and sciences is housed in the 1890s electricity station that once powered Sydney's trams. Exhibits include costumes and jewelry, a whole floor of working steam engines, a pub, space modules, airplanes suspended from the ceiling, state-of-the-art computer gadgetry, and a 1930s art deco–style movie-theater auditorium. Hands-on displays encourage participation, and older children will be intrigued by the opportunities that these present.

A highlight of the museum is the top-level Powerhouse Garden Restaurant, painted in spectacularly vibrant colors and patterns by famous local artist Ken Done and his team. *500 Harris St., Ultimo, tel. 02/9217–0444 or 02/9217–0111. $8. Daily 10–5. www.phm.gov.au*

60 **PYRMONT BRIDGE.** Dating from 1902, this is the world's oldest electrically operated swing-span bridge. The structure once carried motor traffic, but it is now a walkway that links Darling Harbour's east and west sides. The monorail runs above the bridge, but the center span still swings open to allow tall-masted ships into Cockle Bay, the landward portion of Darling Harbour.

63 **SEGA WORLD.** Along with such amusement-park favorites as a roller coaster and a haunted house, the attractions at this vast indoor entertainment park include a wraparound theater, a high-tech adventure playground, and VR-1, a virtual reality ride. The park is divided into three theme zones: past, present, and future. Children ages 8 to 15 love this place. *1–25 Harbour St., Darling Harbour, tel. 02/9273–9273. $28. Weekdays 11–10, weekends 10–10. www.segaworld.com.au*

59 **SYDNEY AQUARIUM.** The city's largest aquarium is a fascinating underwater world, with everything from saltwater crocodiles to

giant sea turtles to delicate, multicolored reef fish and corals. Excellent displays illustrate the marine life of the Great Barrier Reef and Australia's largest river system, the Murray-Darling. Children will particularly enjoy the touch pool and the marine mammal sanctuary with its playful seals. The highlights of the aquarium are two transparent tunnels submerged in an oceanarium. A footpath takes you safely through the water while sharks, eels, and stingrays glide overhead. The aquarium is often very crowded on weekends. *Aquarium Pier, Wheat Rd., Darling Harbour, tel. 02/9262–2300. $17.50. Daily 9:30 AM–10 PM. www.sydneyaquarium.com.au*

SYDNEY CITY CENTER

Most travelers visit Sydney's city center primarily for shopping, but there are several buildings and other places of interest among the myriad office blocks, department stores, and shopping centers.

A Good Walk

Begin at the Market Street end of Pitt Street Mall. Turn left into Market Street and walk a few meters to the entrance to **AMP Tower** ⑥⑥. High-speed elevators will whisk you to the top of the city's tallest structure, and the spectacular view will give you an excellent idea of the lay of the land.

Return to Market Street and walk in the other direction to George Street. Turn left and continue to the Sydney Hilton Hotel, on the left-hand side. For a little refreshment, take the steps down below street level to the Marble Bar, an opulent basement watering hole with extraordinary decor and architecture.

Back up on George Street cross the road to enter the **Queen Victoria Building (QVB)** ⑥⑦, a massive Victorian structure that occupies an entire city block. The shops are many and varied, and the meticulous restoration work is impressive.

After browsing in the QVB, exit at the Druitt Street end and cross this road to the elaborate **Sydney Town Hall** ⑥⑧, the domain of Sydney City Council and a popular performance space. Next door is **St. Andrew's Cathedral** ⑥⑨, Sydney's Anglican church.

Cut across George Street and walk along Bathurst Street to the southern section of **Hyde Park** ⑦⓪. This is the city center's largest green space and the location of the **Anzac War Memorial**, which commemorates Australians who fought and died in the service of their country.

Continue through the park to College Street, cross the road, and walk a few more feet to the **Australian Museum** ⑦①. An excellent natural history museum, it has one of the country's best collections of geological, botanical, and biological specimens from the Australia–Pacific region.

From the museum, cross College Street and then Park Street and follow the shady avenue through the northern half of Hyde Park. This area contains the impressive Archibald Memorial Fountain. Continue past the fountain and cross the road to Macquarie Street. As you walk north on Macquarie, you'll pass the **Hyde Park Barracks, Sydney Mint** and **Sydney Hospital** (☞ Sights to See in Macquarie Street and the Domain South, *above*). In front of the hospital, cross the road to the large pedestrian precinct of **Martin Place** ⑦② and walk the length of the plaza to George Street. Note the impressive Victorian and more recent banks and public buildings, and the cenotaph war memorial near the far end.

From here you can return to the Pitt Street Mall via Pitt Street, or walk north on George Street to Circular Quay.

TIMING

The walk itself should take no longer than a couple hours. Plan more time for an extended tour of the Australian Museum or for shopping in the Queen Victoria Building. Weekday lunchtimes (generally 1–2) in the city center are elbow-to-elbow affairs, with office workers trying to make the most of their brief break.

Sights to See

66 **AMP TOWER.** Short of taking a scenic flight, a visit to the top of this 1,000-ft golden-minaret-topped spike is the best way to view Sydney's spectacular layout. This is the tallest building in the city, and if you come here on a smog-free day, the views from its indoor observation deck are astounding. The panorama encompasses the entire Sydney metropolitan area of more than 1,560 square km (600 square mi), and you can often see as far as the Blue Mountains, more than 80 km (50 mi) away. *100 Market St., between Pitt and Castlereagh Sts., tel. 02/9229–7444. $10, Sun.–Fri. 9 AM–10:30 PM, Sat. 9 AM–11:30 PM. www.centrepoint.com.au*

71 **AUSTRALIAN MUSEUM.** The public face of a well-respected academic institution, the strength of this natural history museum is its collection of plants, animals, and geological specimens from the Asia–Pacific region. The museum has a good collection of artifacts from Papua New Guinea in particular, but much of its vast array of Aboriginal artifacts is not on public display. According to Aboriginal belief, some of the objects are considered sacred and should not be seen by uninitiated men and women. The museum has a comprehensive gems and minerals display, an excellent shop, and a lively café. *6 College St., near William St., tel. 02/9320–6000. $5. Daily 9:30–5. www.austmus.gov.au*

70 **HYDE PARK.** Declared public land by Governor Phillip in 1792 and used for the colony's earliest cricket matches and horse races, this area was made into a park in 1810. Gardens are formal, with fountains, statuary, and tree-lined walks. The park provides some welcome city-center tranquillity and is popular with office workers at lunchtime. *Elizabeth, College, and Park Sts.*

In the southern section of Hyde Park (near Liverpool Street) stands the 1934 Art Deco **Anzac Memorial**. It pays tribute to the

Australians who died in the service of their country during the First World War, when the acronym ANZAC (Australian and New Zealand Army Corps) was coined. The 120,000 gold stars inside the dome represent each man and woman of New South Wales who served in the Great War. The lower level is devoted to an exhibit of war-related photographs. *Hyde Park, tel. 02/9267–7668. Mon.–Sat. 10–4, Sun. 1–4.*

NEED A BREAK? Stop in the **Marble Bar** for a drink, and to experience a masterpiece of Victorian extravagance. The 1890 bar was formerly located in another building that was favored by gentlemen of the racing fraternity. Threatened with demolition in the 1970s, the whole bar was moved—marble arches, colored-glass ceiling, elaborately carved woodwork, paintings of voluptuous nudes, and all—to its present site beneath the Sydney Hilton. By night, it serves as a backdrop for jazz and other live music. *Sydney Hilton Hotel, basement level, 259 Pitt St., tel. 02/9266–0610. Closed Sun.*

72 **MARTIN PLACE.** Sydney's largest pedestrian precinct, flanked by banks, offices, and the MLC Shopping Centre, forms the hub of the central business district. There are some grand buildings here—including the beautifully refurbished Commonwealth Bank and the 1870s Venetian Renaissance–style General Post Office building with its 230-ft clock tower (now a Westin hotel). Toward the George Street end of the plaza the simple 1929 cenotaph war memorial commemorates Australians who died in World War I. Every weekday from about 12:30, the amphitheater near Castlereagh Street is the site for free lunchtime concerts with sounds from all corners of the music world, from police bands to string quartets to rock and rollers. *Between Macquarie and George Sts.*

67 **QUEEN VICTORIA BUILDING.** Originally the city's produce market, this vast 1898 sandstone structure had become a maze

of shabby offices by the time it disappeared under scaffolding in 1981. When the wraps came off five years later, the building was handsomely restored with sweeping staircases, enormous stained-glass windows, and the 1-ton Royal Clock, which is suspended from the glass roof. Other restoration highlights in this 650-ft-long building include the period-style tiling on the ground floor, the central glass dome, and Victorian-era toilets on the Albert Walk level. The QVB is excellent for shopping. The complex includes more than 200 boutiques, with those on the upper floors generally more upmarket and exclusive. The basement level has a variety of inexpensive eating options. *George, York, Market, and Druitt Sts., tel. 02/9264–9209. Daily 24 hrs.*

69 **ST. ANDREW'S CATHEDRAL.** Sydney's Gothic Revival Anglican cathedral (the country's oldest) was founded in 1819 and consecrated in 1868. The church was built with local sandstone and designed by Edmund Blacket, Sydney's most famous church architect. Highlights include the ornamental windows illustrating the life of Christ and the great east window with its images relating to the life of St. Andrew. *Sydney Sq., George St., next to Town Hall, tel. 02/9265–1661. Mon., Tues., Thurs., and Fri. 7:30–5:30; Wed. 7:30 AM–8 PM; Sat. 9–4; Sun. 7:30 AM–8 PM; tours weekdays at 11 and 1:45, Sun. at noon.*

68 **SYDNEY TOWN HALL.** Sydney's most ornate Victorian building—an elaborate, multilayered sandstone structure—is often rather unkindly likened to a wedding cake. The building has some grand interior spaces, especially the vestibule and large Centennial Hall, and performs many functions. The building houses council offices, but is also used as a performance venue for, among others, lunchtime concerts that star the massive Grand Organ, one of the world's most powerful. Tours of the building run from time to time. Call ahead for details. *George and Druitt Sts., tel. 02/9265–9007; 02/9231–4629 for tour information. Weekdays 9–5.*

ELIZABETH BAY AND KINGS CROSS, DARLINGHURST, AND PADDINGTON

This bus and walking tour takes you into some of the city's inner east suburbs and looks at the people's Sydney—from the mansions of the colonial aristocracy and the humble laborers' cottages of the same period to the modernized terrace houses of Paddington, one of Sydney's most charming suburbs. You'll also pass through Kings Cross and Darlinghurst, the best-known nightlife district in the country, and visit the acclaimed Sydney Jewish Museum.

A Good Walk

Begin at the bus stop on Alfred Street, just behind Circular Quay, and catch Bus 311, which leaves from the stop at the Harbour Bridge end of the street. This bus carries a sign reading either RAILWAY VIA KINGS CROSS or RAILWAY VIA ELIZABETH BAY. Ask the driver to drop you off at Elizabeth Bay House and take a seat on the left side of the bus.

You'll wind your way through the city streets to Macquarie Street, past the State Library, the New South Wales Parliament, Hyde Park Barracks, and St. Mary's Cathedral. The bus then follows the curve of Woolloomooloo Bay, where it passes **Harry's Café de Wheels,** a unique Sydney institution, and beneath the bows of naval vessels at the Garden Island Dockyard, the main base for the Australian navy. Visiting ships from other Pacific Ocean navies can often be seen along this wharf.

Just before the Garden Island gates, the bus turns right and climbs through the shady streets of Potts Point and **Elizabeth Bay** to **Elizabeth Bay House** ⑦③, an aristocratic Regency-style mansion. Built some 150 years ago by Alexander Macleay, the colonial secretary, this is one of Australia's finest historic homes.

After a spin through Elizabeth Bay House, continue north to the **Arthur McElhone Reserve** ⑦④ for a pleasant resting spot with harbor glimpses. Take the stone steps leading down from the park to Billyard Avenue. Near the lower end of this street is a walled garden with cypress trees and banana palms reaching above the parapets. Through the black iron gates of the driveway, you can catch a glimpse of Boomerang, a sprawling, Spanish-style villa built by the manufacturer of the harmonica of the same name. Just beyond the house, turn left to **Beare Park** ⑦5, overlooking the yachts in Elizabeth Bay.

Return to Billyard Avenue. Wait at the bus stop opposite the first gate of Boomerang for Bus 311, but make sure that you catch one marked RAILWAY, *not* CIRCULAR QUAY. This bus threads its way through the streets of Kings Cross, Sydney's nightlife district, and Darlinghurst. During the day the Cross is only half awake, although the doormen of the various strip clubs are never too sleepy to lure passersby inside to watch nonstop video shows. Ask the driver to deposit you at the stop near the corner of Darlinghurst Road and Burton Street. From here, the moving and thought-provoking **Sydney Jewish Museum** ⑦6 is just across the road.

After leaving the museum, walk along the remainder of Darlinghurst Road to Oxford Street. Turn left, and on your right about 300 yards up Oxford Street is the long sandstone wall that serves as the perimeter of **Victoria Barracks** ⑦7 and its **Army Museum.** These barracks were built in the middle of the last century to house the British regiments stationed in the colony. The troops were withdrawn in 1870 and replaced by Australian soldiers.

Almost opposite the main entrance to the barracks is the start of **Shadforth Street** ⑦8, along which you'll see fine examples of terrace houses. These are some of the oldest houses in Paddington. Shadforth Street changes its name to Liverpool Street at the intersection with Glenmore Road.

From Shadforth Street turn right onto Glenmore Road, where the terrace houses are even more elaborate. Follow this road past the intersection with Brown Street to the colorful collection of shops known as Five Ways. The **Royal Hotel** (237 Glenmore Rd., Paddington, tel. 02/331–2604) on the far corner has a fine Victorian pub with leather couches and stained-glass windows. It's a good place to stop for something cool to drink. On the floor above the pub there is a balconied restaurant that is popular on sunny afternoons.

Walk up Broughton Street to the right of the Royal Hotel. Turn right at Union Street, left onto Underwood, and right at William Street. You are now among the boutique shops of Paddington, and you may want to spend some time browsing here before completing the walk. On the right, **Sweet William** (4 William St., Paddington, tel. 02/9331–5468) is a shop for chocolate lovers. If you're in the mood, don't miss Oxford Street's offbeat clothing and curio shops.

Walk toward the city along Oxford Street to the restored colonial mansion of **Juniper Hall** ⑲, which marks the end of this tour.

There are buses back to the city from the other side of Oxford Street, but if the sun is shining, consider heading out to Bondi Beach, a mere 20-minute ride on Bus 380.

TIMING

Allow the better part of a day to make your way through these neighborhoods, especially if you have a good look around Elizabeth Bay House and the Sydney Jewish Museum. If you wish to tour Victoria Barracks, take this trip on a Thursday and get there by 10, which probably means going there first and seeing the preceding places in the afternoon.

The walk around Paddington is not particularly long, but some of the streets are steep. This walk can be shortened by continuing along Oxford Street from the Victoria Barracks to Juniper Hall, rather than turning onto Shadforth Street. There is an additional diversion on Saturday, when the famous Paddington Bazaar (☞ Flea Markets in Shopping) brings zest and color to the upper end of Oxford Street.

Sights to See

74 **ARTHUR MCELHONE RESERVE.** Another of the city's welcome havens, the reserve has tree ferns, a gushing stream, a stone bridge over a carp pond, and views up the harbor. *Onslow Ave., Elizabeth Bay. Free. Daily, sunrise–sunset.*

75 **BEARE PARK.** As a rule, local favorites are worth checking out, so it is with this waterfront park. With its pleasant harbor views, it's a favorite recreation spot with Elizabeth Bay locals. The adjoining wharf is often busy with sailors coming and going to their yachts, moored out in the bay. *Off Ithaca Rd., Elizabeth Bay. Free. Daily, sunrise–sunset.*

73 **ELIZABETH BAY HOUSE.** Regarded in its heyday as the "finest house in the colony," this 1835–39 mansion has retained little of its original furniture, but the rooms have been restored in the style of its early life. The most striking feature is an oval-shape salon, naturally lighted through glass panels in a dome roof, with a staircase that winds its way to the upper floor. The colonial secretary Alexander Macleay lived here for only six years before suffering crippling losses in the colonial depression of the 1840s. In return for settling his father's debts, his son William took possession of the house and most of its contents and promptly evicted his father. *7 Onslow Ave., Elizabeth Bay, tel. 02/9356–3022. $6. Tues.–Sun. 10–4:30. www.hht.nsw.gov.au/fmuseums.html*

Much of the densely populated but still-charming harborside suburb of **Elizabeth Bay** was originally part of the extensive Elizabeth Bay House grounds. Wrought-iron balconies and French doors on some of the older apartment blocks give the area a Mediterranean feel. During the 1920s and 1930s this was a fashionably bohemian quarter of the city.

OFF THE BEATEN PATH **HARRY'S CAFÉ DE WHEELS** – The attraction of this dockyard nighttime food stall is not so much the pies and coffee Harry dispenses as the clientele. Harry's is a beloved Sydney institution, and famous opera singers, actors, and international rock-and-roll stars have been spotted here rubbing shoulders with shift workers and taxi drivers. Sampling one of the stall's famous meat pies with peas is a must. 1 *Cowper Wharf Rd., Woolloomooloo.*

79 **JUNIPER HALL.** Built in 1824 by gin distiller Robert Cooper, this Paddington notable was named for the juniper berries used to make the potent beverage. Cooper did everything on a grand scale, and that included raising and housing his family. He built Juniper Hall for his third wife, Sarah, whom he married when he was 46 (she was a mere teenager) and who bore 14 of his 24 children. The house later became an orphanage. It was renovated at considerable public expense and opened as a museum during the 1980s. Due to lack of funds the house is now closed to the public and contains offices. 248 *Oxford St., Paddington.*

PADDINGTON. Most of this suburb's elegant two-story houses were built during the 1880s, when the colony experienced a long period of economic growth following the gold rushes of the 1860s. The balconies are trimmed with decorative wrought iron, sometimes known as Paddington lace, that initially came from England and later was produced in Australian foundries. If you look closely at the patterns, you may be able to distinguish between the rose-and-thistle design that came from England and the flannel-flower, fern, and lyre-bird feather designs made in Australia.

During the depression of the 1890s, Paddington's boom came to an abrupt end. The advent of the automobile and motorized public transport just a few years later meant that people could live in more distant suburbs, surrounded by gardens and trees. Such inner-city neighborhoods as Paddington became unfashionable. The area declined further during the depression of the 1930s, when many terrace houses were converted into low-rent accommodations and most of the wrought-iron balconies were boarded up to create extra rooms.

In the late 1960s inner-city living became fashionable, and many young couples rushed to buy these quaint but dilapidated houses at bargain prices. Renovated and repainted, the now-stylish Paddington terrace houses give the area its characteristic, villagelike charm. Today you can expect to pay at least half a million for a small terrace house.

78 **SHADFORTH STREET.** Built at about the same time as Elizabeth Bay House, the tiny stone houses in this street were assembled to house the workers who built and serviced the ☞ **Victoria Barracks.**

76 **SYDNEY JEWISH MUSEUM.** Combining artifacts with interactive media and audiovisual displays, this museum simultaneously chronicles the history of the Jewish people in Australia and commemorates the 6 million Jews who were killed in the Holocaust. Exhibits are brilliantly arranged on eight levels, which lead upward in chronological order, beginning with the handful of Jews who arrived on the First Fleet in 1788, to the founding of the State of Israel, to survivors of the concentration camps who now live in Australia. *Darlinghurst Rd. and Burton St., Darlinghurst, tel. 02/9360–7999. $6, Mon.–Thurs. 10–4, Fri. 10–2, Sun. 11–5. www.sjm.com.au*

77 **VICTORIA BARRACKS.** Built by soldiers and convicts from 1841 on to replace the colony's original Wynyard Barracks—and still occupied by the army—this vast building is an excellent example of Regency-style architecture. The 740-ft-long sandstone facade is particularly impressive. Most of the area within the walls is taken up by a parade ground, and an army band performs here from 10 every Thursday, when anyone is welcome on a free tour of the complex. Dress uniforms have been abolished in the Australian army, so the soldiers wear their parade-ground dress, which includes the famous slouch hat. The brims of these hats are

cocked on the left side, allowing soldiers to present arms without knocking them off.

The **Army Museum** is on the far side of the parade ground, in the former military prison. Exhibits cover Australia's military history from the early days of the Rum Corps to the Malayan conflict of the 1950s. Its volunteer staff is knowledgeable and enthusiastic, and students of military history will not be disappointed. *Oxford St., Paddington, tel. 02/9339–3000. Museum Thurs. 10–noon, Sun. 10–2:30; barracks tour mid-Feb.–early Dec., Thurs. at 10.*

AROUND SYDNEY

The Sydney area has numerous activities of interest that are well away from the city center and inner suburbs. These include historic townships, the Sydney 2000 Olympics site, national parks in which to enjoy the Australian bush, and wildlife and theme parks that will appeal particularly to children.

Other points of interest are the beaches of **Bondi** and **Manly,** the historic city of **Parramatta,** founded in 1788 and located 26 km (16 mi) to the west, and the magnificent **Hawkesbury River,** which winds its way around the city's western and northern borders. Also within easy reach of the city, the waterside suburb of **Balmain** has an interesting Saturday flea market (☞ Flea Markets in Shopping).

Visiting many of these places by public transport would take a considerable amount of time and effort, so it may be smarter to rent a car or to go with one of the tour operators that offer excursions and day trips (☞ Practical Information).

TIMING

Each of the sights below could easily fill the best part of a day. For those short on time, some tour companies combine visits within a particular area—for example, a day trip west to the Olympic Games site, Australian Wildlife Park, and the Blue Mountains.

87 **AUSTRALIAN WILDLIFE PARK.** Part of the ☞ **Australia's Wonderland** complex, this park delivers close encounters with the widest array of animals of Sydney area parks, including koalas, kangaroos, and other Australian fauna, as well as the chance to view crocodiles and rain-forest birds. Also in the park is the **Outback Woolshed,** where sheep are rounded up and shorn in a 30-minute demonstration of a time-honored Australian tradition. *Wallgrove Rd., Eastern Creek, tel. 02/9830–9100. $9.95; free if you also visit Australia's Wonderland. Daily 9–5.*

87 **AUSTRALIA'S WONDERLAND.** The largest amusement park in the Southern Hemisphere is landscaped and choreographed for total fun. Action ranges from a Ferris wheel to a roller coaster to the ☞ **Australian Wildlife Park.** The complex is in the metropolitan region's west. Admission prices cover all rides and entry fees, including the wildlife park and woolshed. *Wallgrove Rd., Eastern Creek, tel. 02/9830–9100. $37. Daily 10–5.*

82 **BONDI.** In spite of its glorious beach and sparkling views, the suburb of Bondi has only recently acquired social status. Bondi—an Aboriginal word meaning "place of breaking waters"—was developed during the 1920s and '30s. But the spare redbrick architecture, lack of trees, and generally flat terrain did their share to reduce the suburb's appeal. Over the years, Bondi acquired a seedy image fostered by low rents and a free-and-easy lifestyle that the suburb afforded. Author Peter Corris—Australia's Raymond Chandler—used Bondi as a tawdry, neon-lit backdrop for his 1980s thriller, *The Empty Beach.*

During the 1990s, Bondi's proximity to the city and affordable real estate attracted young and upwardly mobile residents. Most of the old apartment blocks have been smartly renovated, and Campbell Parade has been populated with a row of glittering cafés and delicatessens.

Apart from a pleasant day at the beach (☞ South of the Harbor *in* Beaches, *below*), Bondi's main appeal is sociological. This is where Sydney sheds its clothes and most of its inhibitions. Many of the city's sporting subcultures congregate here—among them cyclists, anglers, surfers, bodybuilders, and skateboarders—as does a crowd of exhibitionists and eccentrics. The promenade along the back of the beach is the best place to take all of this in.

To get to Bondi, take Bus 380 or 382 from Circular Quay via Elizabeth and Oxford streets, or catch a train from the city to Bondi Junction and then board Bus 380 or 382. A higher-cost option is the Bondi & Bay Explorer bus (☞ Practical Information).

80 **CENTENNIAL PARK.** Located on the edge of the city's fashionable inner-eastern suburbs, this is Sydney's favorite workout circuit. More than 500 acres of palm-lined avenues, groves of Moreton Bay figs, paperbark-fringed lakes, and cycling and horse-riding tracks make this a popular park. In the early 1800s, the marshy land at the lower end provided Sydney with its freshwater. The park was proclaimed in 1888, the centenary of Australia's foundation as a colony. The Centennial Park Café is often crowded on weekends, but the mobile canteen between the lakes in the middle of the park serves hamburgers, rolls, and espresso. Bikes and blades can be hired from the outlets in nearby Clovelly Road, on the eastern side of the park. *Oxford St. and Centennial Ave., Centennial Park. Daily sunrise–sunset.*

86 **FEATHERDALE WILDLIFE PARK.** Northwest of the city, this park is home to a roll call of Australia's extraordinary fauna in their native bush setting. Even most Australians will never see these creatures in the wild. *217 Kildare Rd., Doonside, tel. 02/9622–1644. $12. Daily 9–5.*

81 **FOX STUDIOS.** Australia's largest movie production facility also incorporates an amusement park, which takes children on a journey into the world of film and television. Center of the action is The Backlot, where the attractions include giant-size models

Speak 'Strine?

Copping an earful of 'strine—to use the local vernacular—is one of the distinct pleasures of a trip here. However, it's becoming increasingly scarce.

In the era of the global village, many of the words that once formed a colorful adjunct to the English language have fallen from popular usage, especially in urban areas, which is where more than 90% of the population lives. Letters to the editor frequently lament the Americanization of the language and that, for example, such trusty and traditional expressions as "blokes" have been largely replaced by "guys." Australians now say, "Get a life," where a decade ago they would have said, "Cop it sweet!" The store assistant who hands you your change is more likely to say, "Have a nice day" than "Farewell," and expressions such as "sheilas" (women) and "fair dinkum" (true) are rarely heard these days except in country pubs.

Australians tend to shorten many common words, and most are easy enough to decipher—"Chrissie" (Christmas), "footsie" (football), and "bikie" (biker), for example. Others, though—such as "postie" (mailman), "cozzie" (swimming costume), and "garbo" (garbage collector)—require some lateral thinking.

Note, however, that it is not essential to have a grasp of 'Strine to travel, eat, and find a bed in Australia. English will serve you perfectly well.

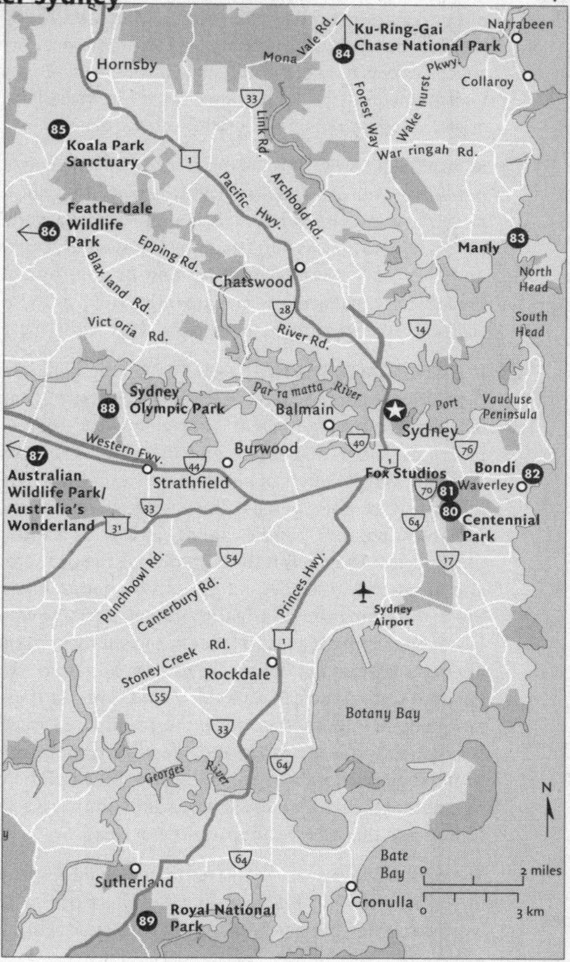

Ku-Ring-Gai Chase National Park
84
Narrabeen
Hornsby
Mona Vale Rd.
Collaroy
Pkwy.
Forest Way
Wake hurst
33
Link Rd.
85
Koala Park Sanctuary
1
War ringah Rd.
Pacific Hwy.
Archbold Rd.
Featherdale Wildlife Park
86
Epping Rd.
Manly
83
North Head
Blax land Rd.
Chatswood
28
Vict oria Rd.
River Rd.
14
South Head
Sydney Olympic Park
88
Par ra matta River
Balmain
Port
Sydney
Vaucluse Peninsula
Western Fwy.
87
Burwood
40
76
Australian Wildlife Park/ Australia's Wonderland
44
Strathfield
1
Fox Studios
Bondi
82
70
81
Waverley
33
31
64
80
Centennial Park
Punchbowl Rd.
54
Princes Hwy.
17
Canterbury Rd.
Sydney Airport
1
Stoney Creek Rd.
Rockdale
55
Botany Bay
33
64
Georges River
N
64
Bate Bay
0
2 miles
Sutherland
Cronulla
0
3 km
89
Royal National Park

of figures from *Star Wars, Planet of the Apes,* and *The X Files.* The biggest attraction of all is "*Titanic*—The Experience," which uses special effects to take the audience through a re-creation of the final moments of the ill-fated liner. *Driver Ave., Moore Park, tel. 1300/369849. $37.95. Daily 10–6. www.foxstudios.com.au*

85 **KOALA PARK SANCTUARY.** At this private park on Sydney's northern outskirts, you can feed and photograph a koala. Cuddling Australia's favorite marsupials is prohibited by state law. The sanctuary also houses dingoes, kangaroos, emus, and wallaroos, and there are sheep-shearing and boomerang-throwing demonstrations. Feeding times are 10:20, 11:45, 2, and 3. *84 Castle Hill Rd., West Pennant Hills, tel. 02/9484–3141. $10. Daily 9–5.*

84 **KU-RING-GAI CHASE NATIONAL PARK.** Originally inhabited by the Guringai Aboriginal tribe, for which the park is named, this is the site of many ancient Aboriginal rock engravings and paintings. The creation of the park in the 1890s also ensured the survival of large stands of eucalypts, as well as small pockets of rain forest in moist gullies. The wildlife here includes swamp wallabies, possums, and goannas, as well as a wide range of bird species. The many trails that traverse the park are a delight and are mostly designed for easy-to-moderate hikes. Among them, the 3-km (2-mi) Garigal Aboriginal Heritage Walk at West Head is recommended, as it takes in ancient rock-art sites. There are many trails in the Bobbin Head area, and from Mt. Ku-ring-gai train station you can walk the 3-km (2-mi) Ku-ring-gai track to Appletree Bay. Another track, the 30-minute Discovery Trail, is negotiable in a wheelchair and offers an excellent introduction to the region's flora and fauna. Leaflets on all of the walks are available at the park's entry stations and from the Kalkari Visitor Centre and the Wildlife Shop at Bobbin Head.

The park is only 24 km (15 mi) north of Sydney. Railway stations at Mt. Ku-ring-gai, Berowra, and Cowan, close to the park's western border, provide access to walking trails. On Sunday, for example, you can walk from Mt. Ku-ring-gai station to Appletree Bay then to Bobbin Head, where a bus can take you to the Turramurra rail station. By car, take the Pacific Highway to Pymble. Then turn into Bobbin Head Road or continue on the highway to Mt. Colah and turn off into the park on Ku-ring-gai Chase Road. Another approach: Follow the Pacific Highway to Pymble and then drive along the Mona Vale Road to Terry Hills and take the West Head turnoff.

Camping in the park is permitted only at the Basin in Pittwater. Sites must be booked in advance (tel. 02/9972–7378). Rates are $15 per night for two people during peak periods and $10 in the off-season. Each additional person is $3 during peak periods and $2 at other times. Children under 5 are free. Supplies can be purchased in Palm Beach.

For more information, contact Ku-ring-gai Chase National Park Visitors Centre. *Box 834, Hornsby 2077, tel. 02/9457–9322 weekdays; 02/9457–9310 weekends.*

83 **MANLY.** Until the Sydney Harbour Bridge was built in the 1930s, Manly's air of distant enchantment and ease made it a popular holiday resort. Many Sydneysiders can still recall childhood holidays spent at Manly, embroidered with sand castles, dribbling ice creams, and visits to the Manly Aquarium and the amusement park on Manly Pier.

A sprawling suburb surrounding the base of North Head, the rearing promontory at the northern approach to Sydney Harbour, Manly has an ocean beach as well as a harbor beach (☞ North of the Harbor in Beaches, *below*). The area was named by Governor Phillip, the colony's first governor, when he noted the "manly behavior" of the local Aborigines. Two years later, in 1790, he might have reconsidered his choice of words when those same Aborigines speared him in the shoulder at Manly Cove.

Manly is more family oriented than Bondi—better mannered, better shaded, and well equipped with cafés—although it does lack its southern sister's sheer entertainment value. If you're thinking about spending the day in Manly, there is also the Quarantine Station (☞ Sights to See in Sydney Harbour, *above*) to visit. To get to Manly, take a ferry or JetCat from Circular Quay. From its landing point the beach is a 10-minute walk.

★ 89 **ROYAL NATIONAL PARK.** Established in 1879 on the coast south of Sydney, the Royal has the distinction of being the first national park in Australia and the second in the world, after Yellowstone National Park in the United States. Originally set aside as a combination botanical and zoological garden for city dwellers, the park remains popular among Sydneysiders on long weekends and holidays. Surprisingly few foreign travelers visit the national park, however. Those who do are guaranteed great bird-watching—more than 200 species have been recorded.

Several walking tracks traverse the park, most of which require little or no hiking experience. The Lady Carrington Walk, a 10-km (6-mi) trek, is a self-guided tour that crosses 15 creeks and passes several historic sites. Other tracks take you along the coast past beautiful wildflower displays and through patches of rain forest. You can canoe the Port Hacking River upstream from the Audley Causeway. Rent canoes and boats at the Audley boat shed on the Port Hacking River.

Royal National Park is 35 km (22 mi) south of Sydney via the Princes Highway to Farnell Avenue (south of Loftus) or McKell Avenue at Waterfall. The Illawarra–Cronulla train line stops at Loftus, Engadine, Heathcote, Waterfall, and Otford stations, where most of the park's walking tracks begin. The park charges a $7.50 entrance fee per vehicle per day.

Although most visitors stay for only a day, campsites are available. Camping facilities at Bonnie Vale Camping Area generally require reservations and deposits at the park visitor center in Audley, especially during school vacations and long weekends. Camping fees are $10 per night for two people and

$2 for each additional person over five years of age. Hot showers, toilets, and laundry facilities are available at the eastern end of Bonnie Vale, 1,650 ft from the campsite. Bush camping is currently forbidden, in order to speed recovery of vegetation affected by the bushfires. Groceries can be purchased in Bundeena, about a mile from the camping area.

Further information is available from the Royal National Park Visitor Centre (Box 44, Sutherland 2232, tel. 02/9542–0648) or from the National Parks and Wildlife Service district office (tel. 02/9542–0666).

88 **SYDNEY OLYMPIC PARK.** Located 14 km (9 mi) west of the city center, this was the focus of events for the 2000 Olympic and Paralympic Games. Sprawling across 1,900 acres on the shores of Homebush Bay, the site was originally a muddy, mangrove-covered backwater on the Parramatta River. By the 1960s, Homebush Bay had served as a racecourse, brick works, armaments depot, and slaughterhouse. During the next decade the bay experienced its ugliest era when it was contaminated through uncontrolled dumping of household and industrial waste, some of it highly toxic.

The transformation has been miraculous. Rising from the shores of the bay is a series of majestic stadiums, arenas, and accommodation complexes. The centerpiece of Olympic Park is the 85,000-seat, $665 million Olympic Stadium. Among the park's vast array of sporting facilities are an aquatic center, archery range, athletic center, tennis center, and velodrome. Since the conclusion of the 2000 Olympic Games, the site has been used for concerts and conferences as well as sporting events.

The Royal Sydney Easter Show, the largest agricultural show in the country, takes place here the two weeks before Easter. The excitement includes displays of rural crafts and produce, animal competitions, and skills demonstrations.

The best way to see Sydney Olympic Park is on an Explorer Bus Tour, operated by Sydney Buses. Explorer Buses leave the Visitor Centre every 20 minutes between 9:30 and 3:30 and travel in a circuit around the site. Passengers can leave the bus at any Explorer Bus stop, stroll around the facility and board any following Explorer Bus. A shuttle bus is available between the Centre and Strathfield Station, reached by train from Town Hall or Central stations. *1 Australia Ave., Homebush Bay, tel. 02/9735–4306. $10. Daily 9–5.*

BEACHES

Sydney is tailor-made for beach lovers. Within the metropolitan area there are more than 30 ocean beaches, all with golden sand and rolling surf, as well as several more beaches around the harbor with calmer water for safe swimming. If your hotel is on the south side of the harbor, the logical choice for a day at the beach is the southern ocean beaches between Bondi and Coogee. On the north side of the harbor, Manly is easily accessible by ferry, but beaches farther north involve a long trip by car or public transport.

Lifeguards are on duty at most of Sydney's ocean beaches during summer months, and flags indicate whether a beach is being patrolled. "Swim between the flags" is an adage that is drummed into every Australian child, with very good reason: The undertow can be very dangerous. Idyllic as it might appear, Sydney's surf claims a number of lives each year, a high proportion of them visitors who are not familiar with local conditions. The flags indicate that a beach is patrolled by lifeguards. If you get into difficulty, don't fight the current. Breathe evenly, stay calm, and raise one arm above your head to signal the lifeguards.

Some visitors to Sydney are concerned about sharks. Although there is no shortage of sharks both inside and outside the harbor, many Sydney beaches are protected by nets, and the risk of shark attack is very low. A more common hazard is jellyfish, known locally as bluebottles, which inflict a painful sting with a risk of death if the sting is not treated quickly. Vinegar is the common remedy, and the staff at most beaches will supply it. Many beaches will post warning signs when bluebottles are present, but you can determine the situation for yourself by looking for the telltale blue bladders washed up along the waterline.

Topless sunbathing is common at all Sydney beaches, but full nudity is permitted only at a couple of locations, including Lady Jane Beach, close to Watsons Bay on the south side of the harbor.

Details of how to reach the beaches by bus, train, or ferry are provided below, but some of the city's harbor and southern beaches are also on the **Bondi & Bay Explorer** bus route (☞ Practical Information). These are Nielsen Park, Camp Cove, Lady Jane, Bondi, Bronte, Clovelly, and Coogee.

Numbers in the margin correspond to beaches on the Sydney Beaches map.

Inside the Harbor

★ ⑩ **BALMORAL.** This long, peaceful beach—among the best of the inner-harbor beaches—is backed by parkland in one of Sydney's most exclusive northern suburbs. The Esplanade, which runs along the back of the beach, has several snack bars and cafés. You could easily combine a trip to Balmoral with a visit to Taronga Zoo (☞ Sydney Harbour, *above*). To reach Balmoral, take the ferry from Circular Quay to Taronga Zoo and then board Bus 238. *Raglan St., Balmoral.*

⑫ **CAMP COVE.** Just inside South Head, this crescent-shaped beach is where Sydney's fashionable people come to see and be seen. The gentle slope of the beach and the relatively calm water make it a safe playground for young children. A shop at the northern

sydney beaches north

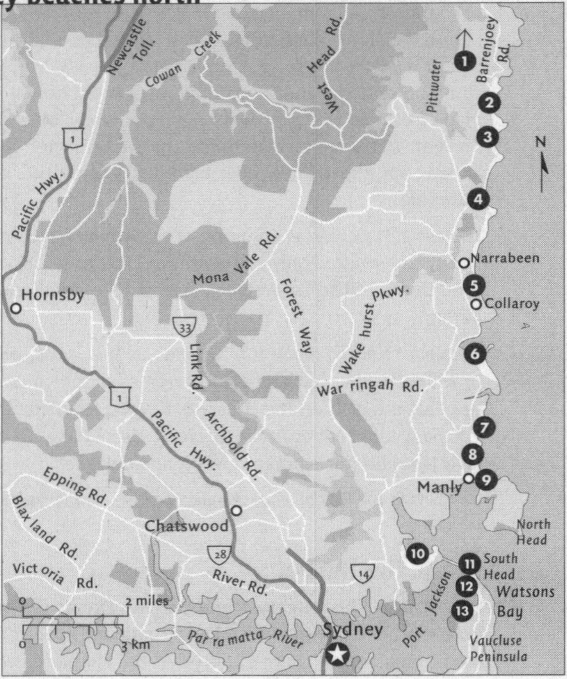

Balmoral, 10
Bungan, 3
Camp Cove, 12
Collaroy–Narrabeen, 5
Dee Why–Long Reef, 6
Freshwater, 7
Lady Jane, 11
Manly, 8
Newport, 2
Nielsen Park, 13
Palm Beach, 1
Shelly, 9
Warriewood, 4

sydney beaches south

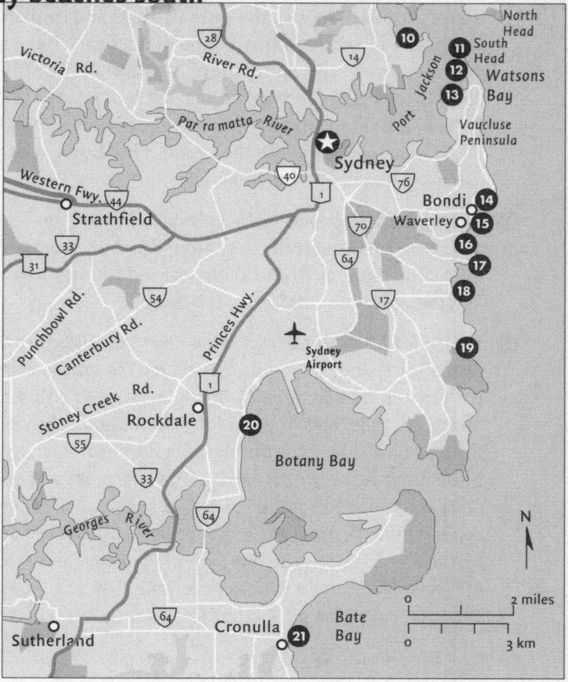

Balmoral, 10
Bondi, 14
Botany Bay, 20
Bronte, 16
Camp Cove, 12
Clovelly, 17
Coogee, 18
Cronulla, 21
Lady Jane, 11
Maroubra, 19
Nielsen Park, 13
Tamarama, 15

end of the beach sells a variety of salad rolls and fresh fruit juices. The grassy hill at the southern end of the beach has a plaque to commemorate the spot where Captain Arthur Phillip, the commander of the First Fleet, first set foot inside Port Jackson. Parking is limited, and if you arrive by car after 10 on weekends, you'll have a long walk to the beach. Take Bus 324 or 325 from Circular Quay. *Cliff St., Watsons Bay.*

⓫ **LADY JANE.** Lady Jane—officially called Lady Bay—is the most accessible of the nude beaches around Sydney. From Camp Cove, follow the path north and then descend the short steep ladder leading down the cliff face to the beach.

⓭ **NIELSEN PARK.** This beach at the end of the Vaucluse Peninsula is small by Sydney standards, but behind the sand is a large, shady park that is ideal for picnics. The headlands at either end of the beach are especially popular for their magnificent views across the harbor. The beach is protected by a semicircular net, so don't be deterred by the correct name of this beach, Shark Bay. The shop and café behind the beach sell drinks, snacks, and meals. Parking is often difficult on weekends. A 10-minute walk will take you to historic Vaucluse House (☞ Sydney Harbour, *above*) and a very different harborside experience. Take Bus 325 from Circular Quay. *Greycliffe Ave. off Vaucluse Rd., Vaucluse.*

South of the Harbor

★ ⓮ **BONDI.** Wide, wonderful Bondi (pronounced *bon*-dye) is the most famous and most crowded of all Sydney beaches. It has something for just about everyone, and the droves who flock here on a sunny day give it a bustling, carnival atmosphere unmatched by any other Sydney beach. Facilities include toilets and showers. Cafés, ice cream stands, and restaurants are on Campbell Parade, which runs behind the beach. Families tend to prefer the more sheltered northern end of the beach. Surfing is popular at the south end, where you'll also find a path that winds along the sea-sculpted cliffs to Tamarama and Bronte beaches.

Take Bus 380 or 382 from Circular Quay via Elizabeth and Oxford streets, or take the train from the city to Bondi Junction and then board Bus 380 or 382. *Campbell Parade, Bondi.*

20 **BOTANY BAY.** Despite this bay's historical association with Captain James Cook, Lady Robinson's Beach, which stretches for several miles along the bay, is bleak, featureless, and close to a major traffic artery. Take Bus 302 or 303 from Circular Quay, or take the train from the city to Rockdale and then board Bus 478. *Grand Parade, Brighton-le-Sands.*

★ 16 **BRONTE.** If you want an ocean beach that is close to the city, has a choice of sand or parkland, and offers a terrific setting, this one is hard to beat. Bronte is surrounded by a wooded park of palm trees and Norfolk Island pines. The park includes a playground and sheltered picnic tables, and excellent cafés are in the immediate area. The breakers can be fierce, but the sea pool at the southern end of the beach offers safe swimming. Take Bus 378 from Central Station, or take the train from the city to Bondi Junction and then board Bus 378. *Bronte Rd., Bronte.*

★ 17 **CLOVELLY.** Swimming is safe at the end of this long, keyhole-shaped inlet, even on the roughest day, which makes it a popular family beach. There are toilet facilities but no snack bars or shops in the immediate area. This is also a popular spot for snorkeling. Take Bus 339 from Argyle Street, Millers Point (the Rocks), or Wynyard bus station; Bus 341 from Central Station; or a train from the city to Bondi Junction. Then board Bus 329. *Clovelly Rd., Clovelly.*

18 **COOGEE.** A reef protects this lively beach (pronounced kuh-jee), creating calmer swimming conditions than those found at its neighbors. A grassy headland overlooking the beach has an excellent children's playground. Cafés in the shopping precinct at the back of the beach sell ice cream, pizza, and the ingredients for picnics. Take Bus 373 from Circular Quay or Bus 372 from Central Station. *Coogee Bay Rd., Coogee.*

21 **CRONULLA.** Even on the hottest day you can escape the crowds at Cronulla, the southernmost and largest beach in the metropolitan area. Good surf is usually running at this beach, and the sand is backed by parkland. Cronulla is a long way from the city by train, however, and its attractions don't justify a long trip for anyone not staying nearby. *Kingsway, Cronulla.*

19 **MAROUBRA.** This expansive beach is very popular with surfers, although anyone looking for more than waves will probably be unimpressed by the rather scrappy surroundings and the lackluster shopping area. Take Bus 395 from Central Station or Bus 396 from Circular Quay. *Marine Parade, Maroubra.*

★ 15 **TAMARAMA.** This small, fashionable beach (it's also known as "Glam-a-rama") is one of Sydney's prettiest, but the rocky headlands that squeeze close to the sand on either side make it less than ideal for swimming. The sea is often hazardous here. A café at the back of the beach sells open sandwiches, fresh fruit juices, and fruit whips. Surfing is not allowed. Take the train from the city to Bondi Junction. Then board Bus 391, or walk for 10 minutes along the cliffs from the south end of Bondi Beach. *Tamarama Marine Dr., Tamarama.*

North of the Harbor

3 **BUNGAN.** If you *really* want to get away from it all, this is the beach for you. Very few Sydneysiders have discovered Bungan, and those who have would like to keep it to themselves. As well as being relatively empty, this wide, attractive beach is one of the cleanest, due to the prevailing ocean currents. Access to the beach involves a difficult hike down a wooden staircase, and there are no facilities. Take Bus 184 or 190 from the Wynyard bus station. *Beach Rd., off Barrenjoey Rd., Mona Vale.*

5 **COLLAROY–NARRABEEN.** This is actually one beach that passes through two suburbs. Its main attractions are its size—it's almost 3 km (2 mi) long—and the fact that it's always possible to escape

the crowds here. The shops are concentrated at the southern end of the beach. Take Bus 155 or 157 from Manly or Bus 182, 184, 189, or 190 from the Wynyard bus station. *Pittwater Rd.*

❻ **DEE WHY–LONG REEF.** Separated from Dee Why by a narrow channel, Long Reef Beach is remoter and much quieter than its southern neighbor. However, Dee Why has better surfing conditions, a big sea pool, and several take-out shops. Take Bus 136 from Manly. *The Strand, Dee Why.*

❼ **FRESHWATER.** This small beach is protected by sprawling headlands on either side, making it popular among families. The surf club on the beach has good facilities as well as a small shop that sells light refreshments. Take Bus 139 from Manly. *The Esplanade, Harbord.*

★ ❽ **MANLY.** The Bondi Beach of the north shore, Manly caters to everyone except those who want to get away from it all. The beach itself is well equipped with changing and toilet facilities. The nearby shopping area, the Corso, is lined with cafés, souvenir shops, and ice cream parlors. Manly also has several nonbeach attractions (☞ Around Sydney, *above*). The ferry ride from the city makes a day at Manly feel more like a holiday than just an excursion to the beach. Take a ferry or JetCat from Circular Quay. From the dock at Manly the beach is a 10-minute walk. *Steyne St., Manly.*

❷ **NEWPORT.** With its backdrop of hills and Norfolk Island pines, this broad sweep of sand is one of the finest of the northern beaches. Within easy walking distance is a shopping center offering one of the best selections of cafés and take-out shops of any Sydney beach. Newport is known for its bodysurfing, and the atmosphere is fairly relaxed. Take Bus 189 or 190 from the Wynyard bus station. *Barrenjoey Rd., Newport.*

❶ **PALM BEACH.** The wide golden sands of Palm Beach mark the northern end of Sydney's beaches. The ocean beach runs along one side of a peninsula separating the large inlet of Pittwater from the Pacific Ocean. Bathers can easily cross from the ocean side to Pittwater's calm waters and sailboats, and you can take a circular ferry trip around this waterway from the wharf on the Pittwater side. The view from the lighthouse at the northern end of the beach is well worth the walk. On a windy day, the southern end of the beach affords some protection. Nearby shops and cafés sell light snacks and meals. The suburb of Palm Beach is a favorite with successful filmmakers and with Sydney's wealthy elite, many of whom own weekend houses in the area. Take Bus 190 from Wynyard bus station. *Ocean Rd., Palm Beach.*

9 **SHELLY.** This delightful little beach is protected by a headland rising behind it to form a shady park, and it is well endowed with food options. The snack shop and restaurant on the beach sell everything from light refreshments to elaborate meals, and there are a couple of waterfront cafés at nearby Fairy Bower Bay. On weekends the beach is crowded and parking in the area is nearly impossible. It's best to walk along the seafront from Manly. Take a ferry or JetCat from Circular Quay to Manly. From there the beach is a half-mile walk. *Marine Parade, Manly.*

4 **WARRIEWOOD.** Enticing and petite in its cove at the bottom of looming cliffs, Warriewood has excellent conditions for surfers and windsurfers. For swimmers and sunbathers, however, the beach does not justify the difficult journey down the steep cliffs. Anyone traveling by public transport faces a long walk from the nearest bus stop. Basic toilet facilities are available on the beach, but there are no shops nearby. Take Bus 184, 189, or 190 from Wynyard bus station or Bus 155 from Manly. *Narrabeen Park Parade, Warriewood.*

Your checklist for a perfect journey

WAY AHEAD
- Devise a trip budget.
- Write down the five things you want most from this trip. Keep this list handy before and during your trip.
- Make plane or train reservations. Book lodging and rental cars.
- Arrange for pet care.
- Check your passport. Apply for a new one if necessary.
- Photocopy important documents and store in a safe place.

A MONTH BEFORE
- Make restaurant reservations and buy theater and concert tickets. Visit fodors.com for links to local events.
- Familiarize yourself with the local language or lingo.

TWO WEEKS BEFORE
- Replenish your supply of medications.
- Create your itinerary.
- Enjoy a book or movie set in your destination to get you in the mood.
- Develop a packing list. Shop for missing essentials. Repair and launder or dry-clean your clothes.

A WEEK BEFORE
- Stop newspaper deliveries. Pay bills.
- Acquire traveler's checks.
- Stock up on film.
- Label your luggage.
- Finalize your packing list—take less than you think you need.
- Create a toiletries kit filled with travel-size essentials.
- Get lots of sleep. Don't get sick before your trip.

A DAY BEFORE
- Drink plenty of water.
- Check your travel documents.
- Get packing!

DURING YOUR TRIP
- Keep a journal/scrapbook.
- Spend time with locals.
- Take time to explore. Don't plan too much.

In This Chapter

THE ROCKS AND CIRCULAR QUAY 87 • French 87 • Italian 88 • Modern Australian 88 • Thai 92 • CITY CENTER AREA 93 • Chinese 93 • French 93 • Malaysian 93 • Modern Australian 94 • Pan-Asian 95 • Steak 95 • EAST SYDNEY AND DARLINGHURST 95 • Cafés 95 • Chinese 96 • French 96 • Modern Australian 97 • Seafood 99 • Thai 99 • KINGS CROSS 100 • Modern Australian 100 • PADDINGTON 100 • Italian 100 • Modern Australian 101 • POTTS POINT 101 • Modern Australian 101 • SYDNEY AREA DINING 102 • Cafés 102 • French 102 • Japanese 103 • Modern Australian 103 • Seafood 107

By Terry Durack

eating out

ALTHOUGH MOST SYDNEY restaurants are licensed to serve alcohol, the few that aren't usually allow you to bring your own (BYOB). Reservations are generally required with a few noticeable exceptions where no bookings at all are taken. Lunch is most often served between noon and 2:30, and dinner is served, usually in a single sitting, between 7 and 10:30. A 10% tip is customary, and there may be a corkage fee in BYOB restaurants, but there is no sales tax or service charge. Some establishments may add a small surcharge on weekends and holidays.

CATEGORY	COST*
$$$$	over $60
$$$	$40–$60
$$	$20–$40
$	under $20

**per person, excluding drinks and tip*

THE ROCKS AND CIRCULAR QUAY

French

$$$$ QUAY. Chef Guillaume Brahimi once cooked with the great Parisian master Joel Robuchon, and if his lush and luscious pommes Parisienne (please don't call them mashed potatoes!) are anything to go by, he has obviously learned his lessons well. Not that he isn't producing a few trademark dishes of his own: His basil-infused tuna is already a Sydney icon, and his slowly roasted whole veal sweetbread served with truffle and an asparagus infusion is a revelation. Brahimi's roasted King Island chicken with foie gras ravioli alone would make Quay worth a visit, even if it didn't enjoy some of Sydney's very best harbor views. *Overseas Passenger Terminal, Circular Quay West, tel. 02/9251–5600. Reservations essential. AE, DC, MC, V. No lunch weekends.*

Italian

$$$$ **AQUA LUNA.** Although Aqua Luna looks out onto the watery charms of Circular Quay, the food harks back to the gently rolling hills of Tuscany. Little wonder, since chef Darren Simpson was previously the head chef of the Italianate Sartoria restaurant in London's Savile Row. Simpson's flavors are rustic, authentic, and whenever possible, organic. Favorites include a salad of artichokes, salted lemons, honey, and almonds; a hearty rabbit-and-borlotti-bean risotto; and succulent wood-roasted blue-eye cod. *Shop 18, 2 Macquarie St., East Circular Quay,, tel. 02/9251–0311. Reservations essential. AE, DC, MC, V. Closed Sun. No lunch Sat.*

$$$$ **BEL MONDO.** Some of Sydney's most refined modern Italian cooking is found in a restored 1913 Rocks district warehouse space that also houses the Argyle Department store. With its glamorous big-night-out feel and dramatic, raised, open kitchen, bel mondo is pure theater. But it's the food, prepared by the talented Manfredi family, that keeps the crowds coming back. Flavors are cool and classy, from a quick antipasto and a spaghetti at the low-key bar to the silky house-made gnocchi with black truffles and delectable preserved ginger panna cotta. *Argyle Department Store, 12–24 Argyle St., Level 3, the Rocks, tel. 02/9241–3700. Reservations essential. AE, DC, MC, V. No lunch Sat.*

Modern Australian

$$$$ **ARIA.** If you were any closer to the Opera House, you'd be in it. After scoring big with the ultracool, black-clad brigade, Chef Matthew Moran and partner Peter Sullivan moved from Moran's in Potts Point to this clubby, lavishly appointed restaurant perched in perfect position on the East Circular Quay waterfront. From the Mercedes Benz upholstery to the Limoges porcelain, everything screams, "Big Night Out!" It's the appropriate setting for Moran's delicate seared sea scallops with creamed corn and Sevruga caviar, lush confit of ocean trout with baba ghanouj, and roasted milk-fed veal rack. *1 Macquarie St., East Circular Quay, tel. 02/9252–2555. Reservations essential. AE, DC, MC, V. Closed Sun. No lunch Sat.*

$$$$ BENNELONG. For reasons too various to list here, the Bennelong has never quite fulfilled the potential of what has to be the most superbly located dining room in the whole city. Yet to eat in one of the modern wonders of the world, surrounded by the undeniable genius of architect Joern Utzon, is still a very special experience. So while some of Sydney's highest profile restaurateurs have come and gone, the crowds still keep coming, and a well-prepared menu of Mediterranean- and French-influenced fare makes sure they keep coming back, as does a well-stocked crustacean bar. *Sydney Opera House, Bennelong Point, tel. 02/9250–7578 or 02/9250–7548. Reservations essential. AE, DC, MC, V. Closed Sun. No lunch.*

$$$$ ★ ROCKPOOL. A meal at Rockpool is a crash course in what modern Australian cooking is all about, conducted in a brave new world of glamorous chrome and glass. Chefs Neil Perry and Kahn Danis weave Thai, Chinese, Mediterranean, and Middle Eastern influences into their repertoire with effortless flair and originality. Prepare to be amazed by herb- and spice-crusted tuna on braised eggplant salad, stir-fried squid with black-ink noodles, slow-cooked abalone with black fungi and truffle oil, and the magnificent Chinese roast pigeon with shiitake-mushroom lasagna. If there's room (and there's always room), try the famous date tart. *107 George St., the Rocks, tel. 02/9252–1888. Reservations essential. AE, DC, MC, V. Closed Sun. No lunch Sat.*

$$$ HARBOURKITCHEN & BAR. Massive changes have swept through this fine-dining restaurant at the Park Hyatt Sydney (☞ Rocks and Circular Quay in Where to Stay). Radically redesigned, reinvented,

Weight Conversion Chart

Kilograms/Pounds

To change kilograms (kg) to pounds (lb), multiply kg by 2.20.
To change lb to kg, multiply lb by .455.

kg to lb	lb to kg
1 = 2.2	1 = .45
2 = 4.4	2 = .91
3 = 6.6	3 = 1.4
4 = 8.8	4 = 1.8
5 = 11.0	5 = 2.3
6 = 13.2	6 = 2.7
7 = 15.4	7 = 3.2
8 = 17.6	8 = 3.6

Grams/Ounces

To change grams (g) to ounces (oz), multiply g by .035.
To change oz to g, multiply oz by 28.4.

g to oz	oz to g
1 = .04	1 = 28
2 = .07	2 = 57
3 = .11	3 = 85
4 = .14	4 = 114
5 = .18	5 = 142
6 = .21	6 = 170
7 = .25	7 = 199
8 = .28	8 = 227

central sydney dining

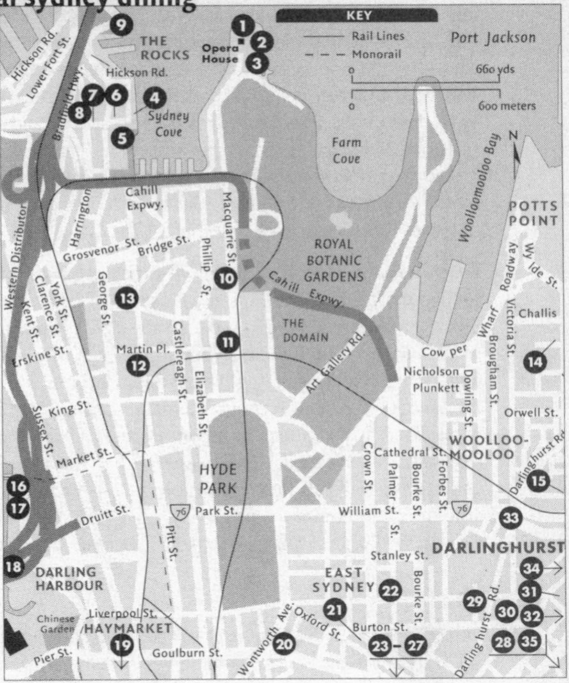

Aqua Luna, 3
Aria, 2
Banc, 11
Bayswater Brasserie, 15
bel mondo, 8
Bennelong, 1
bills, 31
Bistro Mars, 34
bonne femme, 22
Buon Ricardo, 32
Chicane, 21
Chinta Ria Temple of Love, 16
Coast, 17
Dragonfly, 24
Fishface, 29
Forty One, 10
Fu-Manchu, 30
Fuel, 27
Golden Century, 19
harbourkitchen & bar, 9
The Jersey Cow, 35
Longrain, 20
Marque, 23
MCA Café, 5
La Mensa, 28
MG Garage Restaurant, 26
Paramount, 14
Prasit's Northside on Crown, 25
Prime, 12
Quay, 4
Rockpool, 7
Sailor's Thai, 6
Salt, 33
The Summit, 13
Wockpool, 18

and renamed, it has swallowed up much of the ground floor of the hotel in one broad curve. Dramatic harbor views are democratically shared by this one-size-fits-all restaurant and its attendant bars. The food, under ex-Rockpool chef Ross Lusted, is best described as Modern Rustic. Pan-roasted mussels are steamy and succulent, spit-roasted baby chicken is crisp and golden-skinned, and char-grilled swordfish steak with corn cakes is worth taking your eyes off the view for a few minutes at least. *7 Hickson Rd., The Rocks, tel. 02/9256–1660. Reservations essential. AE, DC, MC, V.*

$$ MCA CAFÉ. Neil Perry, of Rockpool fame, walks across the road to this smart café tucked into the Museum of Contemporary Art. Snare an umbrella-shaded table on the neat terrace (ask when you book), and you'll enjoy sweeping views of the Opera House and Circular Quay. That might be Sydney Harbour out there, but the food is full of Mediterranean sunshine, running from simple pasta dishes to the golden tarragon-roasted chicken breast or the thick, grilled tuna steak Ligurian-style. When you've finished you can always walk off lunch with a leisurely stroll through the adjoining contemporary art gallery. *140 George St., the Rocks, tel. 02/9241–4253. Reservations essential. AE, DC, MC, V. No dinner.*

Thai

$$$ SAILOR'S THAI. This glamorously restored restaurant in the Old Sailors Home in the Rocks district serves up some of Sydney's most exciting and authentic Thai food. Local business types rub shoulders with sightseers and hard-core shoppers while lapping up delicious red curries and salads fragrant with lime juice and fish sauce. More unusual treats include a succulent pineapple-and-cashew-nut stir-fry and a delicious caramelized venison with coriander seeds. Upstairs is a casual noodle bar, its long, communal stainless-steel table groaning with offerings such as *som dtam* (shredded papaya salad) and *kanom jeem* noodles. *106 George St., the Rocks, tel. 02/9251–2466. Reservations essential. AE, DC, MC, V. Closed Sun. No lunch Sat.*

CITY CENTER AREA

Chinese

$$ **GOLDEN CENTURY.** For two hours—or as long as it takes for you to consume delicately steamed prawns, luscious mud crab with ginger and shallots, and *pipis* (triangular clams) with black bean sauce—you're in Hong Kong. This place is a seafood heaven, with wall-to-wall fish tanks filled with crab, lobster, abalone, and schools of barramundi, parrot fish, and coral trout. You won't have to ask if the food is fresh. Most of it is swimming around you as you eat. The atmosphere is no-frills and the noise level can be deafening, but the eating is very good. Supper is served from 10 until 3. *393–399 Sussex St., Haymarket, tel. 02/9212–3901. AE, DC, MC, V.*

French

$$$ **BANC.** Dashing restaurateur-about-town Stan Sarris and British-trained chef Liam Tomlin have joined forces to turn a former bank into the city center's most lavish dining room, complete with marble columns, high ceilings, and sleek, two-toned banquettes. Throw in a 22-page wine list, a heavily laden cheese trolley, and a legal-eagle lunch crowd, and you have the city's most seductive dining scene. It's made even more enticing by an ethereally light scallop mousse with sauteed scampi, roast squab, and the ultimate lemon tart. *53 Martin Pl., tel. 02/9233–5300. Reservations essential. AE, DC, MC, V. Closed Sun. No lunch Sat.*

Malaysian

$$ ★ **CHINTA RIA TEMPLE OF LOVE.** Part-time jazz DJ Simon Goh puts a unique spin on Malaysian restaurants. His latest effort features a giant laughing Buddha, miked-up chefs, and retro furniture salvaged from a car-factory canteen. The music is loud and swinging, much like the crowds that flock here. The no-reservations policy means you need to get here early to be sure of a table. Waits

can be lengthy, even on Monday nights. Still, the coconut-rich curry *laksa*, fiery *blachan* spinach, flaky curry puffs, and Hokkien *mee* noodles are worth the wait. *Roof Terrace, Cockle Bay Wharf, Darling Park, tel. 02/9264–3211. AE, DC, MC, V.*

Modern Australian

$$$$ **FORTY ONE.** The view of Sydney from the 41st floor is glamorous and glorious, the private dining rooms are lush and plush, and Dietmar Sawyere's Asian-influenced classical food is full of flair and finesse. Especially recommended is the dramatically presented crown roast of hare with Indian spices, along with the tantalizing warm salad of Chinese duck and sea scallops, and the cruelly delicious Valrhona chocolate tart. The restaurant's decadent Krug Room is a snug haven for those who still believe a glass of champagne and a little foie gras can cure most of the world's ills. *Chifley Tower, Level 41, 2 Chifley Sq., tel. 02/9221–2500. Reservations essential. AE, DC, MC, V. Closed Sun. No lunch Sat.*

$$$$ ★ **THE SUMMIT.** Fun dining is replacing fine dining in Sydney. Nowhere is this more obvious than the Summit, a 30-year-old revolving restaurant once famous for its all-you-can-eat buffets. Under culinary visionary Anders Ousback, the Summit has been reborn and is now the darling of the see-and-be-seen black-clad brigade. As Sydney revolves around you at a meter a minute, go retro and order the prawn cocktail followed by duck à l'orange, or stay true to the times with goose-liver parfait with Tokay jelly and ocean trout with bone marrow and pinot butter. *Level 47, Australia Square, 264 George St., tel. 02/9247–9777. Reservations essential. AE, DC, MC, V.*

$$$ **COAST.** Swish new waterside complexes and good dining don't always go hand in hand, but Coast is just one of several very good eateries that have made Cockle Bay Wharf one of Sydney's most enjoyable eating areas. The place is pure Sydney with its vaguely nautical good looks, sunny outdoor terrace, and sparkling water views. The food is typical Sydney bistro: deep-fried calamari with

aioli; simply grilled reef fish of the day with pink-eye potatoes and lemon oil; and rack of lamb with roast eggplant, tomato, and pesto. *Roof Terrace, Cockle Bay Wharf, Darling Park, tel. 02/9267–6700. AE, DC, MC, V.*

Pan-Asian

$$$ **WOCKPOOL.** In the heart of tourist-laden Darling Harbour, Wockpool glows and shimmers like a futuristic Pan-Asian space station. Filmy silk hangs from the ceiling, and the whole place has a rakish, Philippe Starck sense of the modern about it. The brainchild of Rockpool's Neil Perry, Wockpool started life as a wired-up, streetwise noodle bar in nearby Potts Point, but soon moved to this large space on the ground floor of the Panasonic Imax Theatre. Chef Claudia Dunlop presents modern Asian cooking at its most glamorous and fluent, such as a seductive stir-fried crab omelet and gloriously sticky caramelized pork. *Southern Promenade, Darling Harbour, tel. 02/9211–9888. Reservations essential. AE, DC, MC, V.*

Steak

$$$$ **PRIME.** Until Prime came along, steak houses in Sydney were old-fashioned, macho affairs where men in dark suits scoffed down copious quantities of cheap red wine and charred red meat. Inspired by the likes of Smith & Wollensky and Maloney & Porcelli in New York, Stan Sarris, of Banc fame, decided to lift the image of the Aussie steak. This is an elegant restaurant located in the basement of the recently renovated city post office. As well as serving some of the best steaks in town, Prime also offers knockout seafood tortellini and poached barramundi with clams. *1 Martin Pl., tel. 02/9229–7777. Reservations essential. AE, DC, MC, V. Closed Sun. No lunch Sat.*

EAST SYDNEY AND DARLINGHURST

Cafés

$ ★ **BILLS.** This sunny corner café is so addictive it should come with a health warning. It's a favorite hangout of everyone from local nurses to semi-disguised rock stars, and you never know who you might be sitting next to (isn't that Tom Cruise?) at the big communal table. If you're not interested in the creaminess of what have to be Sydney's best scrambled eggs, try the ricotta hot cakes with honeycomb butter. At lunch you'll have to decide between the spring-onion pancakes with gravlax and the most famous steak sandwich in town. *433 Liverpool St., Darlinghurst, tel. 02/9360–9631. Reservations not accepted. No credit cards. BYOB. Closed Sun. No dinner.*

Chinese

$ FU-MANCHU. With its bright red stools, shiny red chopsticks, stainless-steel communal tables, and light, cutting-edge design, you'd almost expect fussy, fashionable fusion food. But Fu-Manchu keeps to simple, no-fuss stir-fries, noodle dishes, and Chinese roast meats. The wonton noodle soup with red roasted pork is heaven in a bowl, the Peking duck wraps are handheld delights, and the northern-style dumplings are the real thing. *249 Victoria St., Darlinghurst, tel. 02/9360–9424. Reservations not accepted. No credit cards. BYOB.*

French

$$$ MARQUE. Six years ago, Mark Best won an award as Sydney's most promising young chef. Now that early promise has been fulfilled with the opening of his sleek and elegant Darlinghurst restaurant. Few people approach French flavors with such passion and dedication. Stints with three-star demigods Alain Passard, in Paris, and Raymond Blanc, in England, haven't done any harm either, and it's impossible not to be impressed when food is this well crafted. Best's boned chicken with pearl barley farce is a triumph. Ditto the salad of autumn vegetables and the baby madeleines. *355 Crown St., Surry Hills, tel. 02/9332–2225. Reservations essential. AE, DC, MC, V. Closed Sun. No lunch.*

Modern Australian

$$$$ ★ MG GARAGE RESTAURANT. Surry Hill's MG Garage has Sydney all revved up: This glamorous good-time restaurant is also a sports-car showroom. High performance chef Janni Kyritsis has wowed 'em at Berowra Waters and the Bennelong. Here, he pleases palates with an amazing salmon *coulibiac* (with rice, eggs, shallots, and mushrooms and wrapped in a brioche pastry shell); roast pigeon-and-cabbage rolls with a liver, heart, and pork stuffing; and rosebud parfait with pear, orange, and sour cherries. *490 Crown St., Surry Hills, tel. 02/9383–9383. Reservations essential. AE, DC, MC, V. Closed Sun. No lunch Sat.*

$$$ CHICANE. If looks count for anything, this slick Darlinghurst newcomer is sure to make an impression on the Sydney bar-and-restaurant scene. With its good-looking design, good-looking crowd, and good-looking food, you can't help but feel that you're making the place look untidy unless you're built like an Adonis, deeply tanned, and drop-dead gorgeous like just about everyone else here. Still, the staff is friendly, the scene rarely dies before 2, and the food ranges from good to great with standouts including red emperor fillet with broad-bean cassoulet and spring lamb Dijonnaise with savoy cabbage. *1a Burton St., Darlinghurst tel. 02/9380–2121. AE, DC, MC, V. No lunch.*

$$$ SALT. Are you wearing black? Is your hand in martini position? Do you look like someone groovy and influential? Then you're ready to dine at Salt, the hippest, happiest Mod Oz bistro, where the customers look as if they've stepped out of a Bret Easton Ellis novel. Chef Luke Mangan has worked with three-star chefs in London, and his skills shine in dishes such as the tea-smoked duck breast with pomegranate and oyster mushrooms, and salt-baked salmon with celery and vanilla stock, peas, and asparagus. *229 Darlinghurst Rd., Darlinghurst tel. 02/9332–2566. Reservations essential. AE, DC, MC, V.*

$$ BONNE FEMME. In the middle of bustling Darlinghurst, bonne femme is tucked away like a little oasis of calm. If you're not looking for it, you could easily pass it by without noticing, which would be a shame since British-born Andrew Turner is one of Sydney's more promising young chefs. The space is confident—high on detail, low on fuss—much like Turner's cooking, which runs from a rich and refined chicken liver parfait with Madeira jelly to a hearty dish of tender pork cheeks with garlic and sage. Don't miss the tarte Tatin for dessert. *191–193 Palmer St., East Sydney, tel. 02/9331–4455. Reservations essential. AE, DC, MC, V. Closed Mon. No lunch Sat.–Tues.*

$$ DRAGONFLY. If you wondering what a sushi-deli-noodle bar is when it's at home, you're going to have a lot of fun finding out. Young caterers Yuey Then and Anthea Wright either couldn't decide which one to do, or seriously believe the inner urban Surry Hillbillies are ready for a dear little shop-front eatery that specializes in just about everything. Try deliciously fresh California rolls, roast duck and rice noodle soup, and wok-fried Chinese greens and lamb fillet with blue cheese and baby spinach. You can also get mixed sushi to go. If that's not enough, they also do espresso. *478 Bourke St., Surry Hills, tel. 02/9380–7333. Reservations essential. MC, V. Closed Sun. No lunch Mon.–Tues.*

$$ FUEL. Located next door to its more glamorous sibling, the MG Garage, Fuel is a real chip off the old engine block. Like MG, the place doubles as a sports-car showroom with the odd Lotus and Lamborghini scattered around, but the place is far more low-key and far more relaxed. While superchef Janni Kyritsis writes the menus, his young protégé, Jacob Brown, adds his own style and more than a little class to dishes including a nice and homey spaghetti and meatballs; a thick, hearty Greek lima bean soup; and a very Mod Oz squid salad with salt pork. Pick up some gourmet goodies on the way out from Fuel's supercharged food store. *466-488 Crown St., Darlinghurst, tel. 02/9383–9388. Reservations not accepted. AE, DC, MC, V.*

Seafood

$$ **FISHFACE.** Don't expect sea views here. In fact, the largest nearby body of water is to be found at the Laundromat a block or two up the road. Nevertheless, Fishface specializes in some of the freshest, best-value seafood in town. It's a cozy, street-smart sort of place full of fashionably thin types who don't mind waiting for one of the six tables. Paul Wrightson's limited menu depends on what didn't get away that morning and might include steamed red Jewfish, swordfish with mash, and a with-the-works bouillabaisse. *132 Darlinghurst Rd., Darlinghurst, tel. 02/9332–4803. Reservations not accepted. No credit cards. BYOB. No lunch Mon.–Sat.*

Thai

$$$ ★ **LONGRAIN.** Start with a cocktail in the cool, minimalist cocktail bar, where Sydney's high life gathers around low-slung tables. Then make for the dining room, where the hip crowd jostles for a position at one of three giant wooden communal tables. It might be trendy, but the food here is terrific. Chef Martin Boetz approaches Thai cooking with an enthusiasm that's matched by an intimate knowledge of his ingredients. His pomelo-and-cashew salad bursts with freshness, a lacy eggnet omelet filled with prawn and pork is a treasure, and the yellow curry of chicken is rich and gutsy. *85 Commonwealth St., Surry Hills, tel. 02/9280–2888. Reservations not accepted. AE, DC, MC, V. Closed Mon. No lunch weekends.*

$$ **PRASIT'S NORTHSIDE ON CROWN.** Owner Prasit Prateeprasen is the pied piper of pork, peppercorns, and pad Thai, opening restaurants about as often as most of us open newspapers. But these days, Sydney's golden-haired boy seems to be settling down. Now in its fifth year, his most ambitious and successful restaurant has a reassuring air of permanence about it. The place is buzzy and loud, with equally vivid gold-and-purple decor to match. The food makes most suburban Thai restaurants look like, well, suburban Thai restaurants. The lamb *masaman* curry and stuffed blue swimmer crab are heartily recommended. *413 Crown*

St., Surry Hills, tel. 02/9319–0748. Reservations essential. AE, DC, MC, V. BYOB. Closed Sun. No lunch Mon.–Wed. and Sat.

KINGS CROSS

Modern Australian

$$$ ★ **BAYSWATER BRASSERIE.** The Bayz, as regulars affectionately call it, has been serving oysters, colorful cocktails, and easygoing Mediterranean- and Asian-influenced cuisine since 1982. Though food trends, like the staff, have come and gone, the Bayz hasn't missed a beat. Start with a drink in the moody back bar. Then try for a table in the front room, styled like a French brasserie. The menu changes regularly, but there is always an excellent selection of oysters opened to order. Blackboard specials may include braised beef cheeks with polenta or a red curry of chicken with Jasmine rice. *32 Bayswater Rd., Kings Cross, tel. 02/9357–2177. Reservations not accepted. AE, DC, MC, V. Closed Sun.*

PADDINGTON

Italian

$$$ ★ **BUON RICORDO.** Walking into this happy, bubbly place is like turning up at a private party in the backstreets of Naples. Host, chef, and surrogate uncle Armando Percuoco invests classic Neapolitan and Tuscan techniques with inventive personal touches to produce dishes like warmed figs with Gorgonzola and prosciutto, truffled egg pasta, and scampi with saffron sauce and black-ink risotto. Everything comes with Italian style that you can see, feel, smell, and taste. Leaving the restaurant feels like leaving home. *108 Boundary St., Paddington, tel. 02/9360–6729. Reservations essential. AE, DC, MC, V. Closed Sun.–Mon. No lunch Tues.–Thurs.*

$$ **LA MENSA.** Steve Manfredi, of the highly fashionable bel mondo, went down-market (but only just) and across town to open this smart, modern café/food shop with celebrity wholesaler Barry McDonald. Its pressed-metal surfaces, park-bench seating, and windows

thrown open to the street give the place an irresistibly chic but informal air. Food runs from filled baguettes and homey soups to generous pastas and inventive salads. And if you think you'll still feel like eating later on, you can always shop for olive oil, jams, pastas, and confections to take away. 257 *Oxford St., Paddington, tel. 02/9332–2963. Reservations not accepted. AE, DC, MC, V.*

Modern Australian

$$$ **THE JERSEY COW.** Don't let the old milk cans outside the door, the pasture-green carpet, and the rustic cow sketches fool you. The Cow is no hokey theme restaurant. It's an up-to-the-minute Sydney bistro powered by the big-hearted cooking of British-born Darryl Taylor. Trained under London legend Garry Rhodes, with stints under some of the finest chefs in Britain and Sydney, Taylor produces big luscious peasant flavors that practically leap off the plate. Try his Catalonian-style tuna, rabbit-and-quail terrine with winter savory, and cherry clafoutis (a creamy custard flan with sour cherries on top) with roast-almond ice cream. 152 *Jersey Rd., Woollahra, tel. 02/9328–1600. Reservations essential. AE, DC, MC, V. Closed Sun. No lunch.*

POTTS POINT

Modern Australian

$$$$ ★ **PARAMOUNT.** Christine Manfield, the high priestess of Mod Oz cooking, has no shortage of believers at her glamorous, softly glowing Potts Point restaurant. It's a cozy space, all curves and swerves and softness, full of bright, good-looking food and bright, good-looking people. You'll love the choices, especially the grilled sea scallops with chili salt squid and black-ink noodles; soy-braised, corn-fed chicken; and brandied-cherry-and-coconut trifle. Manfield's natty, curved-edge cookbooks have made her something of a celebrity in Sydney food circles. Pick one up while you're here. 73 *Macleay St., Potts Point, tel. 02/9358–1652. Reservations essential. AE, DC, MC, V. No lunch.*

SYDNEY AREA DINING

Cafés

$$$ **SEAN'S PANAROMA.** It may look like a cross between a half-finished bomb shelter and a neglected shore house, but this beachside café is home to Sean Moran, one of Sydney's brightest and most innovative young chefs. Weekend breakfasts feature legendary offerings of fruit smoothies and eggs any which way, and lunches are easygoing affairs. At night, things get a little more serious as Moran cooks up memorable dishes including Barossa Valley chicken with sweet-potato puree and peas; braised barramundi with olives, lemon, and spinach; and raspberry, blackberry, and blueberry trifle. *270 Campbell Parade, Bondi Beach, tel. 02/9365–4924. Reservations essential. MC, V. BYOB. Closed Mon.–Tues. in winter. No lunch weekdays. No dinner Sun.*

French

$$$$ **CLAUDE'S.** Chef Tim Pak Poy seems barely old enough to have absorbed all of the craft and technique he exhibits with his startlingly executed and thoughtfully presented food. The restaurant is tiny and unprepossessing, proving that good things really do come in small, plainly wrapped packages. While the cuisine is basically French, Pak Poy allows the best local produce and his own flights of fancy to shine through. Claude's is now licensed, but you may still bring your own fine bottle to accompany such creations as grilled breast of Muscovy duck in caramel, jellied quail with grapes and shredded pigeon salad, and white coffee parfait with raspberries and ginger. *10 Oxford St., Woollahra, tel. 02/9331–2325. Reservations essential. AE, MC, V. Closed Sun.–Mon. No lunch.*

$$$ **BISTRO MARS.** The ponytailed Neil Perry may be more known for his stylish, modern takes on Asian and Mediterranean flavors, yet he cooks French bistro classics as if he grew up in the Sixth Arrondissement of Paris. In his hands, classics such as poached egg in a red wine sauce, warm salad of goose leg, daube of beef shin, and roast saddle of hare take on a new fashionability, without sacrificing an iota of flavor. The room is basically a hotel dining room, yet it is functional, clean lined, and nice enough. The adjoining Café Fish serves all-day café food as well as very good, very fresh fish. *Rushcutters Harbourside Hotel, 100 Bayswater Rd., Rushcutters Bay, tel. 02/9361–3000. Reservations essential. AE, DC, MC, V.*

$$$ **BISTRO MONCUR.** After building Claude's into a gastronomic jewel, Damien Pignolet went around the corner to open a loud and proud bistro that spills over with happy-go-lucky patrons who don't mind waiting a half hour for a table. Here it is relaxing in itself to watch others enjoying the food. How refreshing to order salmon and get salmon, to order sausages and get sausages, and to have no disappointments. Even the coffee at the end of the meal is the ultimate coffee. And the bill, though not cheap, is appropriate to the bistro nature of the place. *Woollahra Hotel, 116 Queen St., Woollahra, tel. 02/9363–2519. Reservations not accepted. AE, DC, MC, V. Closed Mon.*

Japanese

$$ **SHIMBASHI SOBA.** If you're lucky you might catch Yoshi Shibazaki making noodles by hand in his glass-fronted workroom, in the front window of this popular eatery. Shibazaki is one of only 50 chefs recognized by the Japanese government as a master of *soba* (buckwheat noodles) and *udon* (thick wheat noodles). The cold soba noodles with dipping sauce make a refreshing summertime dish. Nabeyaki udon hot pot and beef sukiyaki with udon are year-round crowd pleasers. For a special treat, call ahead to order the Shimbashi hot pot of udon, chicken, prawn, eel, salmon, and more. *Grosvenor and Young Sts., Neutral Bay, tel. 02/9908–3820. AE, DC, MC, V. Closed Sun.–Mon.*

Modern Australian

$$$$ **CATALINA ROSE BAY.** To experience the essential Sydney in a single meal, head straight for Catalina. Every night here resembles a glittering charity premiere as famous personalities toy with

Australian Cuisine

Australia didn't have time to wait for a homegrown cuisine to evolve in the traditional way: by the time the country was settled by the British, it was impossible for it to call upon its own resources without outside influence.

So we borrowed an Anglo-Saxon way of eating that had little to do with where we happened to be. The vast landmass of Australia means that somewhere in the country is a microclimate that will produce whatever we feel like eating. It also didn't take us long to realize that a country surrounded by water is surrounded by oysters, crabs, lobsters, and fish.

The next great influence came from the Southern Europeans who came to this country as refugees after World War II. Many were Spaniards, Greeks, and Italians, people whose lives and foods had been warmed by the Mediterranean sun.

But a truly identifiable Australian way of eating emerged when we realized that it was actually Asia's doorstep we were on. The new Australian cuisine has many faces: Dishes can immortalize indigenous produce, such as steamed barramundi with soy and ginger, or transform more universal ingredients, as in a checkerboard ice-cream flavored with aniseed and pineapple.

But Australian cuisine is no slammed-together grab bag of fusion techniques. It's not about ingredients. It's about attitude. It's brash, easygoing, fresh, and thoroughly natural. It's Tetsuya Wakuda's impossibly silky ocean trout confit with trout roe and konbu seaweed at Tetsuya's in Sydney. Or Sydneysider Neil Perry's adventure trek of mud crab, sweet pork, and green papaw salad at Rockpool.

This is the sort of cooking that has made Australia a modern culinary force. Let the academics ponder if it is a true cuisine or just a lifestyle. The rest of us will do the only sensible thing: head off to a great Australian restaurant and make up our own minds.

—Terry Durack

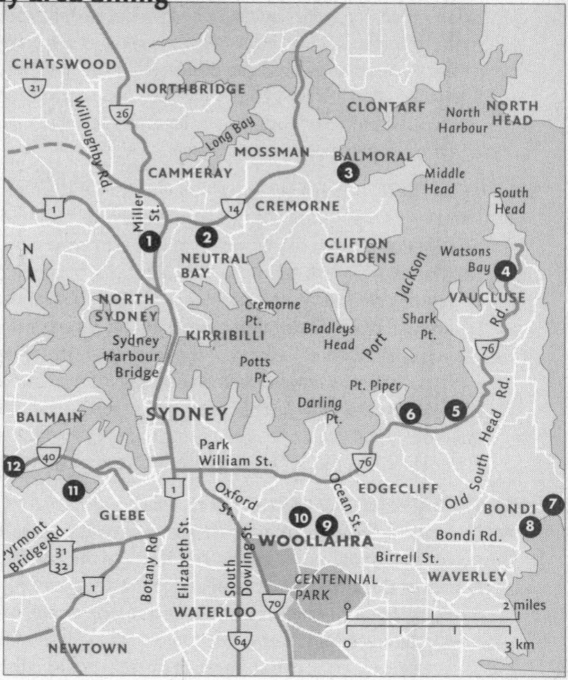

The Bathers' Pavilion, **1**

Bistro Moncur, **9**

Boathouse on Blackwattle Bay, **11**

Catalina Rose Bay, **5**

Claude's, **10**

Doyle's on the Beach, **4**

Hugo's, **7**

Pier, **6**

Sean's Panaroma, **8**

Shimbashi Soba, **3**

Tetsuya's, **12**

calamari cooked in its own ink, red mullet with ratatouille, and made-to-order sushi platters. By day, all eyes are on the harbor as boats, seaplanes, and the odd pelican drift by. Bright, light, and white, this is a gorgeously modern restaurant bustling with gorgeously modern food. *1 Sunderland Avenue, Lune Park, Rose Bay, tel. 02/9371–0555. Reservations essential. AE, DC, MC, V.*

$$$$ ★ **TETSUYA'S.** Tetsuya Wakuda has won three different awards naming his restaurant the finest in Sydney, so it shouldn't come as any surprise that dinner reservations are booked two months in advance. It's worth getting on the waiting list or coming for lunch to sample Wakuda's unique blend of Western techniques and Japanese flavors. The dining room is totally unassuming with its plain, sensible good looks, and the food is breathtaking. Dishes such as wondrous slow-cooked ocean trout, ostrich carpaccio, and blue cheese *bavarois* (a cold custard dessert) leave other chefs gasping. *729 Darling St., Rozelle, tel. 02/9555–1017. Reservations essential. AE, DC, MC, V. Closed Sun.–Mon. No dinner Sat.*

$$$ ★ **THE BATHERS' PAVILION.** Balmoral Beach is blessed. Not only does it possess an inviting sandy beach and great water views, but it also boasts one of the best eating strips north of the Harbour Bridge. Queen of the strip is the completely renovated and rejuvenated Bathers' Pavilion, which includes a restaurant, a café, and a lavish private dining room. Former Regent Hotel executive chef, Serge Dansereau, cooks with one hand on the seasons and the other on the very best local ingredients, producing food that is colorful, light, and thoroughly appropriate to its time and place. *4 the Esplanade, Balmoral, tel. 02/9969–5050. AE, DC, MC, V.*

$$$ **BOATHOUSE ON BLACKWATTLE BAY.** When Sydneysiders talk about "the bridge," they're not necessarily referring to Sydney Harbour. Almost as loved is very much newer Anzac Bridge, which you can see best from a window table at this waterside eatery. You also get a good view of the fish markets, appropriate since seafood is the focus here, with clams, mussels, crabs, and lobsters all

coming from live tanks in the kitchen. Meat eaters can console themselves by ordering beef fillet with pea puree or suckling pig with grilled figs. *End of Ferry Rd., Glebe, tel. 02/9518–9011. Reservations essential. AE, MC, V. Closed Mon.*

$$ HUGO'S. Snappy leisure wear and "cool dude" dispositions are the order of the day at Hugo's, and that's just the waitstaff. Like Bondi itself, this restaurant works effortlessly on many levels, without ever taking itself too seriously. Weekend breakfasts are legendary, especially if you can snag one of the outside bench seats so you can watch the waves as well as the passing parade of gorgeous suntans. At night, things get serious with the justly famous pan-fried prawn and avocado stack, roasted duck breast on bok choy, and spanner crab linguine. *70 Campbell Parade, Bondi Beach, tel. 02/9300–0900. Reservations essential. AE, DC, MC, V. No lunch weekdays.*

Seafood

$$$ DOYLE'S ON THE BEACH. After the Harbour Bridge and the Opera House, an alfresco lunch of fish-and-chips at Doyle's ranks as one of Sydney's most popular tourist draws. Views across the harbor are spectacular, people-watching is first-rate, and on a sunny day, a chilled glass of sauvignon blanc and a dozen oysters are hard to beat. During the weekday lunch hour the restaurant operates its own water taxi. *11 Marine Parade, Watsons Bay, tel. 02/9337–2007. Reservations essential. DC, MC, V.*

$$$ PIER. With its wraparound harbor views and shipshape good looks, this restaurant is a highly appropriate place to enjoy Australia's finest seafood. Chefs Steve Hodges and Greg Doyle know their fish, and manage to reach beyond the predictable char-grills and fish-and-chips without being gimmicky. The freshness of the produce itself sings in such fishes as curried blue-eye cod, pot-roasted rock lobster, and John Dory fillet with English spinach. *594 New South Head Rd., Rose Bay, tel. 02/9327–6561. Reservations essential. AE, DC, MC, V.*

In This Chapter

DEPARTMENT STORES 109 • DUTY-FREE SHOPS 109 • FLEA MARKETS 110 • SHOPPING CENTERS AND ARCADES 111 • SPECIALTY STORES 112 • Aboriginal Art 112 • Books 112 • Bush Apparel and Camping and Outdoor Gear 113 • CDs and Tapes 113 • Crafts 113 • Knitwear 114 • Opals 114 • T-Shirts and Beachwear 115

Updated by Michael Gebicki

shopping

SYDNEY IS AUSTRALIA'S shopping capital. Some of the finest souvenirs are to be found in the city's Aboriginal art galleries, opal shops, crafts galleries, or weekend flea markets. If you're interested in buying genuine Australian products, look carefully at the labels. Stuffed koalas and kangaroos made in Taiwan have become a standing joke in Australia.

DEPARTMENT STORES

DAVID JONES. "Dee Jays," as it's known locally, is the largest department store in the city, with a reputation for excellent service and high-quality goods. Clothing by many of Australia's finest designers is on display here, and the store also markets its own fashion label at reasonable prices. The basement level of the men's store is a food hall with a range of treats from all over the world. *Women's store, Elizabeth and Market Sts.; men's store, Castlereagh and Market Sts., tel. 02/9266–5544. Mon.–Wed. and Fri. 9–6, Thurs. 9–9, Sat. 9–5, Sun. 11–5.*

GRACE BROS. Opposite the Queen Victoria Building, this is the place to shop for clothing and accessories by Australian and international designers. The café on the bookstore level is a great place to rest and recover. *George and Market Sts., tel. 02/9238–9111. Mon.–Wed. and Fri. 9–6, Thurs. 9–9, Sun. 11–5.*

DUTY-FREE SHOPS

Since the federal government reduced the tax that Australians pay on electrical and electronic items to 10%, most goods on sale in duty-free stores are no longer a bargain. The exceptions are tobacco products and alcohol, which still cost far less than in other stores. To shop in a duty-free store, you need a ticket to leave Australia and a passport. Although you can purchase your goods at any time, collect them from the shop 48 hours before you leave. You must carry the goods, which are sealed in plastic carrier bags, on the plane or ship as hand luggage, and you cannot open them until you clear customs.

ALLDERS DUTY FREE. This Circular Quay store sells a wide selection of jewelry, liquor, electronics, and clothing. 22 Pitt St., *tel. 02/9241–5844.*

ANGUS AND COOTE. Sydney's specialist jeweler offers a wide selection of duty-free watches and gemstones. *496 George St., tel. 02/9267–1363. Mon.–Sat. 10–6, Sun. 12:30–6.*

DOWNTOWN DUTY FREE. With two city outlets, Downtown is popular among airline flight crews, who are generally a reliable indicator of the best prices. *Strand Arcade, basement level, off* Pitt St. *Mall, tel. 02/9233–3166;* 105 Pitt St., *tel. 02/9221–4444. Mon.–Wed. 9–5:30, Thurs. 9–8:30, Sat. 9–5, Sun. 11–4.*

FLEA MARKETS

BALMAIN MARKET. This Saturday market, set in a leafy churchyard less than 5 km (3 mi) from the city, has a rustic appeal that is a relaxing change from city-center shopping. The 140-odd stalls display jewelry and some unusual and high-quality bric-a-brac craftwork. Inside the church hall you can buy a truly international range of snacks, from Indian samosas to Indonesian satays to Australian meat pies. *St. Andrew's Church, Darling St., Balmain. Sat. 8:30–4.*

PADDINGTON BAZAAR. Popularly known as Paddington Market, this busy churchyard bazaar has stalls crammed with essential oils and tribal jewelry. Despite its New Age feel, it's a great place to shop for children's clothing and T-shirts at bargain prices. The market is also an outlet for a handful of avant-garde but unknown dress designers, whose clothing is still affordable. The market is a lively, entertaining environment that acts as a magnet for buskers and some of the flamboyant characters of the area. While you're in the neighborhood, check out Oxford Street's cafés and clothing boutiques. *St. John's Church, Oxford St., Paddington. Sat. 10–4.*

THE ROCKS MARKET. Weekends, this sprawling covered bazaar transforms the upper end of George Street into a cultural collage of music, food, arts, crafts, and entertainment. *Upper George St., near Argyle St., the Rocks. Weekends 10–5.*

SHOPPING CENTERS AND ARCADES

HARBOURSIDE. This complex contains more than 200 clothing, jewelry, and souvenir shops. However, its popularity is not so much due to the stores as to its striking architecture and spectacular waterside location. Open daily, the shopping center has many cafés, restaurants, and bars that overlook the harbor. *Darling Harbour.*

PITT STREET MALL. In the heart of Sydney's shopping area, this mall includes the Mid-City Centre, Centrepoint Arcade, Imperial Arcade, Skygarden, Grace Bros., and the charming and historic Strand Arcade—six multilevel shopping plazas crammed with more than 450 shops, most of which sell clothing. *Between King and Market Sts.*

QUEEN VICTORIA BUILDING. A sprawling example of Victorian architecture near Town Hall, the QVB contains more than 200 boutiques, cafés, and antiques shops. Even if you have no intention of shopping, the meticulously restored 1890s building itself is worth a look. The QVB is open 24 hours a day, although the shops do business at the usual hours. *George, York, Market, and Druitt Sts., tel. 02/9264–9209.*

SPECIALTY STORES

Aboriginal Art

Aboriginal art includes functional items, such as boomerangs and spears, as well as paintings and ceremonial implements that testify to a rich culture of legends and dreams. Although much of this artwork remains strongly traditional in character, the tools and colors used in Western art have fired the imaginations of many Aboriginal artists. The two outstanding sources of Aboriginal art are Arnhem Land and the Central Desert Region, which are close to Darwin and Alice Springs, respectively.

ABORIGINAL ART CENTRES. This chain of variously named shops sells Aboriginal work, from large sculpture and bark paintings to such small collectibles as carved emu eggs. *Aboriginal and Tribal Art Centre, 117 George St., Level 1, the Rocks, tel. 02/9247–9625; Aboriginal Art Shop, Opera House, Upper Concourse, tel. 02/9247–4344; 7 Walker Lane, Paddington, tel. 02/9360–63839. Mon.-Wed. and Fri. 9–5:30, Sat. 9–5, Sun. 10–4.*

COO-EE ABORIGINAL ART. A wide selection of wearable Aboriginal artwork includes jewelry and T-shirts painted with abstract designs, sold at moderate prices. *98 Oxford St., Paddington, tel. 02/9332–1544. Mon.–Sat. 10–6, Sun. 11–5.*

Books

ARIEL BOOKSELLERS. This large, bright browser's delight at the lower end of Paddington is the place to go for anything new or avant-garde. It also has the best collection of art books in Sydney. *42 Oxford St., Paddington, tel. 02/9332–4581. Daily 10 am–midnight; and 103 George St., the Rocks, tel. 02/9241–5622. Daily 10–6*

DYMOCKS. Big, bustling, and packed to its gallery-level coffee shop, this midcity bookstore is the place to go for all literary needs. *424–430 George St., tel. 02/9235–0155. Mon.–Wed. and Fri. 9–5:30, Thurs. 9–9, weekends 9–4.*

THE TRAVEL BOOKSHOP. Stop in here for Sydney's most extensive range of maps, guides, armchair travel books, and histories. *Shop 3, 175 Liverpool St., tel. 02/9261–8200. Weekdays 9–6, Sat. 10–5, Sun. noon–5.*

Bush Apparel and Camping and Outdoor Gear

MOUNTAIN DESIGNS. Located in the middle of Sydney's rugged row of outdoor specialists, this store sells the serious camping and climbing hardware necessary to keep you alive and well in the wilderness. *499 Kent St., tel. 02/9267–3822. Mon.–Wed. 9–5:30, Thurs. 9–9, Fri. 9–6, Sat. 9–5, Sun. 10–4.*

PADDY PALLIN. For serious bush adventurers heading for the Amazon, Annapurna, or wild Australia, Paddy's should be the first stop. You'll find maps, books, and mounds of gear tailored especially for the Australian outdoors. *507 Kent St., tel. 02/9264–2685. Mon.–Wed. 9–5:30, Thurs. 9–9, Fri. 9–6, Sat. 9–5, Sun. 10–4.*

R. M. WILLIAMS. This is the place to buy your trendy Australian country wear, including an Akubra hat, Drizabone riding coat, plaited kangaroo-skin belt, and moleskin trousers. *389 George St., tel. 02/9262–2228. Mon.–Wed. and Fri. 9–5:30, Thurs. 9–9, Sat. 9–4, Sun. 10–4.*

CDs and Tapes

FOLKWAYS. If you're looking for a range of Australian bush, folk, and Aboriginal records, Folkways has an especially impressive selection. *282 Oxford St., Paddington, tel. 02/9361–3980. Mon. 9–6, Tues.–Wed. and Fri. 9–7, Thurs. 9–9, Sat. 9:30–6:30, Sun. 10–5.*

Crafts

AUSTRALIAN CRAFTWORKS. Many of the wares here—superb woodwork, ceramics, knitwear, and glassware, as well as small souvenirs made by leading Australian crafts workers—are displayed in the cells of this former police station. *127 George St., the Rocks, tel. 02/9247–7156. Fri.–Wed. 9–7, Thurs. 9–9.*

OBJECT GALLERY. Located inside the refurbished Customs House building, this store sells beautiful creations in glass, wood, ceramic. *31 Alfred St., tel. 02/9247–7318. Weekdays 10–5:30, weekends 10–5.*

Knitwear

DORIAN SCOTT. A wide range of Australian knitwear for men, women, and children includes bright, bold high-fashion garments as well as sweaters and scarves in natural colors. *105 George St., the Rocks, tel. 02/9247–4090. Weekdays 9:30–7, Sat. 9:30–6, Sun. 10–6.*

Opals

Australia has a virtual monopoly on the world's supply of this fiery gemstone. The least expensive stones are doublets, which consist of a thin shaving of opal mounted on a plastic base. Sometimes the opal is covered by a quartz crown, in which case it becomes a triplet. The most expensive stones are solid opals, which cost anything from a few hundred dollars to a few thousand. Opals are sold at souvenir shops all over the city, but anyone who intends to buy a valuable stone should visit an opal specialist.

FLAME OPALS. Selling nothing but solid opals, set in either sterling silver or 18-karat gold, the shop has a wide selection of black, white, and Queensland boulder opals, which have a distinctive depth and luster. The sales staff is very helpful. *119 George St., the Rocks, tel. 02/9247–3446. Weekdays 9–7, Sat. 10–5, Sun. 11:30–5.*

GEMTEC. This is the only Sydney opal retailer with total ownership of its entire production process—mines, workshops, and showroom—making prices very competitive. In the Pitt Street showroom, you can see artisans at work cutting and polishing the stones. *51 Pitt St., Sydney, tel. 02/9251–1599. Weekdays 9–5:30, weekends 10–4.*

T-Shirts and Beachwear

KEN DONE GALLERY. Prominent artist Ken Done catches the sunny side of Sydney with vivid colors and bold brushstrokes. His shop sells a variety of practical products with his distinctive designs, including bed linens, sunglasses, beach towels, beach and resort wear, and T-shirts. *1 Hickson Rd., the Rocks, tel. 02/ 9247–2740. Weekdays 10–5:30, weekends noon–5.*

In This Chapter

Cricket 117 • Football 118 • Golf 118 • Running 118 • Sailing and Boating 119 • Scuba Diving 119 • Surfing 119 • Tennis 120 • Windsurfing 120

Updated by Michael Gebicki

outdoor activities and sports

WHETHER IT'S WATCHING or playing, Sydneysiders are devoted to their sport, and the city's generally benign climate makes outdoor sporting activity a year-round possibility. There are some 80 golf courses within easy reach of the city. Many of these are open to the public, and greens fees are modest compared with those of most countries. Tennis is also popular, with dozens of centers hiring out courts for both day and night use.

By far the most popular summer sport is cricket; Australia plays international test matches at the legendary Sydney Cricket Ground. The biggest winter game is Rugby League, but Rugby Union, soccer, and Australian Rules football also have substantial followings. Many of these winter matches take place at the Sydney Football Stadium.

Cricket

For Australians, the pinnacle of excitement is The Ashes, when the Australian national cricket team takes the field against the English. It happens every other summer (December–January), and the two nations take turns hosting the event. Cricket season runs from October through March. The Ashes is next scheduled for Australia in 2002–03.

Football

Rugby League, known locally as footie, is Sydney's winter addiction. This is a fast, gutsy, physical game that bears some similarities to North American football, although the action is more constant and the ball cannot be passed forward. The season falls between April and September. The **Sydney Football Stadium** (Moore Park Rd., Paddington, tel. 02/9360–6601 for stadium for match information and ticket sales) is the main venue.

Golf

More than 80 golf courses lie within a 40-km (25-mi) radius of the Sydney Harbour Bridge, 35 of which are public. Golf clubs and carts are usually available for rent, but caddies are not.

Bondi Golf Club is a nine-hole public course on the cliffs overlooking famous Bondi Beach. While the par-28 course is hardly a challenge for serious golfers, the views are inspiring. The course is open to the public after noon on most days. *5 Military Rd., North Bondi, tel. 02/9130–1981. Greens fee $12.*

New South Wales Golf Course is a rigorous, challenging, par-72 championship course on the cliffs at La Perouse, overlooking Botany Bay. The course is generally open to nonmembers midweek, but visitors must make advance arrangements with the pro shop. *Henry Head, La Perouse, tel. 02/9661–4455. Greens fee $100.*

A 90-minute drive northwest of Sydney, **Riverside Oaks Golf Club** is a spectacular 18-hole, par-73 course in a classic bush setting on the banks of the Hawkesbury River. *O'Brien's Rd., Cattai, tel. 02/4560–3299. Greens fee weekdays $65, weekends $80.*

Running

One of the finest paths in the city is the route from the **Opera House to Mrs. Macquarie's Chair,** along the edge of the harbor,

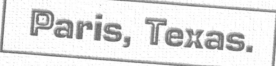

through the Royal Botanic Gardens. At lunchtime on weekdays, this track is crowded with corporate joggers.

In the eastern suburbs, a running track winds south along the cliffs from **Bondi Beach to Tamarama.** It is marked by distance indicators and includes a number of exercise stations.

The **Manly** beachfront is good for running. If you've got legs for it, you can run down to Shelly Beach, or pop over the hill to Freshwater Beach and follow it all the way to check out Curl Curl's huge waves.

Sailing and Boating

At **Eastsail,** near Kings Cross, you can rent, for about $95 per half day, a small boat to sail or motor yourself around the harbor. It's also possible to charter a skippered yacht for a full day's excursion for around $1,500. *D'Albora Marine, New Beach Rd., Rushcutters Bay, tel. 02/9327–1166.*

The **Northside Sailing School** at Middle Harbour rents out small sailboats. Rates start at $20 per hour, and you can also book an instructor to show you the ropes. *The Spit, Mosman, tel. 02/9969–3972.*

Scuba Diving

Pro Dive offers courses and shore- or boat-diving excursions around the harbor and city beaches. Some of the best dive spots are close to the eastern suburbs' beaches of Clovelly and Coogee, where Pro Dive is based. A full day out with an instructor or dive master costs around $100, including rental equipment. *27 Alfreda St., Coogee, tel. 02/9665–6333.*

Surfing

All Sydney surfers have their favorite breaks, but you can usually count on good waves south of Bondi. North of the harbor, stay between Manly and Newport. In summer, surfing reports are a regular feature of radio news broadcasts. That's Sydney (☞ Beaches in Here and There).

Tennis

Cooper Park Tennis Centre is a complex of eight synthetic grass courts in a park surrounded by bush about 5 km (3 mi) east of the city center. *Off Suttie Rd., Cooper Park, Double Bay, tel. 02/9389–9259. Weekdays 7–5 $16 per hr, 5–10 $19 per hr; weekends 8–5 $18 per hr, 5–10 $20 per hr.*

Parklands Sports Centre has nine courts set in a shady park approximately 2½ km (1½ mi) from the city center. *Lang Rd. and Anzac Parade, Moore Park, tel. 02/9662–7033. Weekdays 8–5 $15 per hr, 6 AM–9 PM $17 per hr; weekends 8–6 $17 per hr.*

Windsurfing

The bays and inlets of Sydney Harbour afford great windsurfing opportunities, and **Rose Bay Aquatic Hire** rents out windsurfers for $35 per hour. Hobie Cats and Lasers rent for $30 per hour and up. *1 Vickery Ave., Rose Bay, tel. 02/9371–7036. $20 per hr, high-performance board $35. Oct.–Mar., daily during daylight, weather permitting.*

Distance Conversion Chart

Kilometers/Miles

To change kilometers (km) to miles (mi), multiply km by .621.
To change mi to km, multiply mi by 1.61.

km to mi	mi to km
1 = .62	1 = 1.6
2 = 1.2	2 = 3.2
3 = 1.9	3 = 4.8
4 = 2.5	4 = 6.4
5 = 3.1	5 = 8.1
6 = 3.7	6 = 9.7
7 = 4.3	7 = 11.3
8 = 5.0	8 = 12.9

Meters/Feet

To change meters (m) to feet (ft), multiply m by 3.28.
To change ft to m, multiply ft by .305.

m to ft	ft to m
1 = 3.3	1 = .30
2 = 6.6	2 = .61
3 = 9.8	3 = .92
4 = 13.1	4 = 1.2
5 = 16.4	5 = 1.5
6 = 19.7	6 = 1.8
7 = 23.0	7 = 2.1
8 = 26.2	8 = 2.4

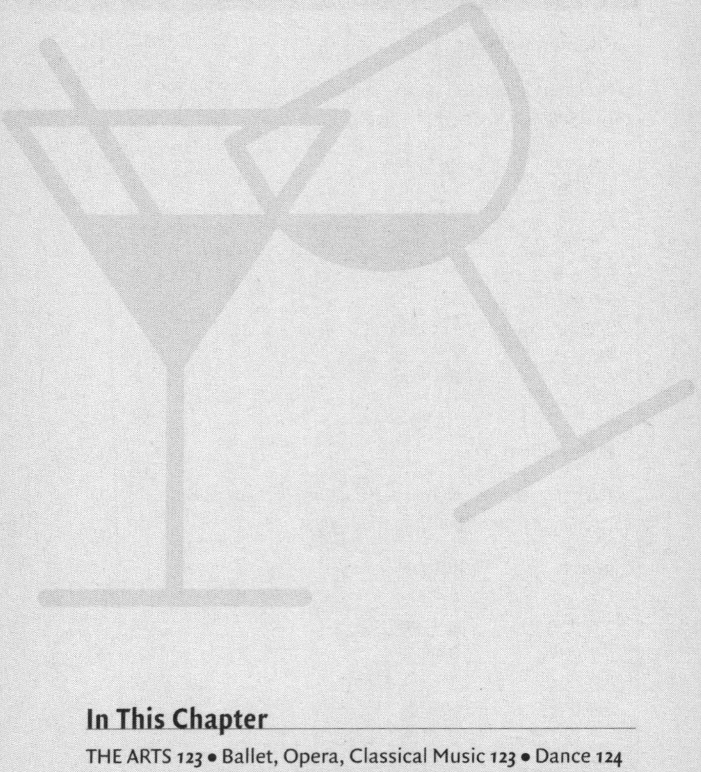

In This Chapter

THE ARTS *123* • Ballet, Opera, Classical Music *123* • Dance *124* • Theater *124* • NIGHTLIFE *125* • Comedy Clubs *126* • Gambling *126* • Gay Bars and Clubs *127* • Jazz Clubs *127* • Nightclubs *128* • Pubs with Music *129*

Updated by Michael Gebicki

nightlife and the arts

THE OPERA HOUSE IS NOT JUST for decoration—nor is it just for opera. Its concert hall and many stages host a number of prominent orchestras and dance and theater companies. Sydney's theater scene is no less impressive. See a performance of the Australian Ballet at the Opera House or a show at The Wharf Theatre, and then continue on to The Cross, Sydney's district of decadence, or happening Oxford Street. Grab a drink and some jazz at The Basement and end up in The Cauldron: Sydney's scene will entertain for as long as you can stay up.

THE ARTS

The most comprehensive listing of upcoming events is in the "Metro" section of the *Sydney Morning Herald* published on Friday. On other days, browse through the entertainment section of the paper. Tickets for almost all stage presentations can be purchased through **Ticketek** agencies. For credit-card bookings (AE, DC, MC, V) call the **Ticketek Phone Box Office** (tel. 02/9266–4800).

BALLET, OPERA, CLASSICAL MUSIC

SYDNEY OPERA HOUSE. Despite its name, this famous building is actually a showcase for all the performing arts: It has five theaters, only one of which is devoted to opera. The Opera House is the home of the Australian Ballet and the Sydney Dance Company, as well as the Australian Opera Company. The complex also includes two stages for theater and the 2,700-seat Concert Hall, where the Sydney Symphony Orchestra and the Australian Chamber Orchestra perform regularly. *Bennelong Point, tel. 02/9250–7777. Box office Mon.–Sat. 9–8:30.*

DANCE

BANGARRA DANCE THEATRE. This Aboriginal dance company stages productions based on contemporary Aboriginal social themes, often to critical acclaim. The company usually performs in its headquarters in the Rocks. *Wharf 4, 5 Hickson Rd., Walsh Bay, tel. 02/9251–5333.*

SYDNEY DANCE COMPANY. Innovative contemporary dance is the specialty of this internationally acclaimed group, who generally perform at the Opera House when they are not touring outside Sydney. *Pier 4, Hickson Rd., Walsh Bay, tel. 02/9221–4811.*

THEATER

BELVOIR STREET THEATRE. The two stages here are home to innovative and challenging political and social drama. Upstairs, under the direction of Neil Armfield, the repertoire is stylish and cerebral. The smaller downstairs space hosts fringe theater and comedy. The theater is a 10-minute walk from Central Station. *25 Belvoir St., Surry Hills, tel. 02/9699–3444.*

CAPITOL THEATRE. The 100-year-old Capitol building, which fell into disrepair during the 1980s, has been revived thanks to a mid-1990s makeover that included such refinements as fiber-optic ceiling lights that twinkle in time to the music. The 2,000-seat theater specializes in Broadway blockbusters, such as *West Side Story* and *My Fair Lady*. *13 Campbell St., Haymarket, tel. 02/9266–4800.*

HER MAJESTY'S THEATRE. Contemporary and comfortable, this theater on the fringe of Chinatown is the most likely place to see mainstream Broadway musicals. *107 Quay St., Haymarket, tel. 02/9212–3411.*

LYRIC THEATRE. The Star City entertainment complex's 2,000-seat theater is Sydney's latest performing arts venue, and despite its size, there is no better place to watch the big budget musicals that are its staple fare. Sight lines are excellent and the configuration is lavishly spacious. *20–80 Pyrmont St., Pyrmont, tel. 02/9777–9000.*

STABLES THEATRE. Regarded as a proving ground for up-and-coming talents and plays, this small theater specializes in avant-garde works that sometimes graduate to the big stage. *10 Nimrod St., Kings Cross, tel. 02/9361–3817.*

STATE THEATRE. The grande dame of Sydney theaters, this midcity venue demands a dressed-up night to pay homage to a golden era. Built in 1929 and restored to its full-blown opulence in 1980, the theater's Gothic foyer features a vaulted ceiling, mosaic floors, marble columns and statues, and brass and bronze doors. A highlight of the magnificent theater is the 20,000-piece chandelier that is supposedly the world's second largest. *49 Market St., tel. 02/9373–6655.*

THE WHARF THEATRE. Located on a redeveloped wharf in the shadow of Harbour Bridge, this is the home of the Sydney Theatre Company, one of the most original and highly regarded companies in Australia. Contemporary British and American plays and the latest offerings from leading Australian playwrights such as David Williamson and Nick Enright are the main attractions. *Pier 4, Hickson Rd., Walsh Bay, tel. 02/9250–1777.*

NIGHTLIFE

"Satan made Sydney," wrote Mark Twain, quoting a citizen of the city, and there can be no doubt that Satan was the principal architect behind **Kings Cross.** Strictly speaking, Kings Cross refers to the intersection of Victoria Street and Darlinghurst Road, although the name "The Cross" applies to a much wider area. Essentially, it is a quarter-mile stretch of bars, burlesque shows, cafés, video shows, and massage parlors. The area does not come to life much before 10 PM, and the action runs hot for most of the night.

Sydneysiders in search of late-night action are more likely to head for Oxford Street, between Hyde Park and Taylor Square, where the choice ranges from pubs to the hottest discos in town. Oxford Street is also the nighttime focus for Sydney's large gay population.

The entertainment section published daily in the *Sydney Morning Herald* is the most informative guide to current attractions in the city's pubs and clubs. For inside information on the club scene—who's been seen where and what they were wearing—pick up a free copy of *Beat*, available at just about any Oxford Street café.

COMEDY CLUBS

THE COMEDY CELLAR AT LANDED. Located in a new shopping complex, this pub is also a music venue, yet it's the Friday- and Saturday-night comedy acts that draw the crowds. *2 Bay St., Glebe, tel. 02/9212–3167. $12–$15. Fri.–Sat. 8:30.*

SYDNEY'S ORIGINAL COMEDY STORE. Sydney's oldest comedy club has relocated to a plush 300-seat theater in the vast movie production facility at Fox Studios. The theater is rather difficult to find. It's located at the rear of the studio complex, close to the parking lot. *Fox Studios, Moore Park, tel. 02/9564–3900. $15. Tues.–Sat. 8.*

GAMBLING

STAR CITY CASINO. This glitzy, Las Vegas–style casino has 200 gaming tables and 1,500 slot machines. Gambling options include roulette, craps, blackjack, baccarat, and the classic Australian game of two-up. *20–80 Pyrmont St., Pyrmont, tel. 02/9777–9000. Daily 24 hrs.*

GAY BARS AND CLUBS

ALBURY HOTEL. A longtime anchor to Sydney's gay scene, this popular pub still draws the crowds with its muscle-bound barmen and nightly drag shows. It's usually the first port of call for gay visitors. *6 Oxford St., Paddington, tel. 02/9361–6555. Daily 2–2.*

BEAUCHAMP HOTEL. This gay pub is mostly remarkable for what it lacks. There are no floor shows, no cruisy lighting, and no dance floor or cocktail bar—just a comfortable, unpretentious, traditional Australian pub that appeals mostly to older gays. *267 Oxford St., Darlinghurst, tel. 02/9331–2575. Daily 10 AM–1 AM.*

MIDNIGHT SHIFT. A perennial favorite with the leather-and-denim set, this gay nightclub is known for its thrashing, high-energy music and laser-light show, which occupy the upper level. Downstairs is a quieter pub that is a popular meeting spot for predinner or after-work drinks. Formerly a men-only bastion, the club is now increasingly popular with lesbians. *85 Oxford St., Darlinghurst, tel. 02/9360–4463. $10. Mon.–Thurs. 9–3, Fri.–Sat. 10–6, Sun. 11–6.*

JAZZ CLUBS

THE BASEMENT. Close to the waterfront at Circular Quay, this subterranean club is the city's premier venue for top Australian and overseas jazz, blues, and funk musicians. Dinner is also available. *29 Reiby Pl., Circular Quay, tel. 02/9251–2797. $5–$20. Weekdays 4:30–midnight, weekends 7–midnight.*

HARBOURSIDE BRASSERIE. With the lights of Harbour Bridge twinkling in the background, this nightclub is a popular place to dine while listening to music. The entertainment varies from rock to world music, but the club is best known as a contemporary jazz venue. A wide range of food, from light snacks to steaks with all the trimmings, is available until midnight. *Pier 1, Hickson Rd., Walsh Bay, tel. 02/9252–3000. $5–$20. Tues.–Sun. usually 7–3.*

ROUND MIDNIGHT. In this cool, sleek, well-mannered club, suits, live music, and martinis remain the order of the day, despite the surrounding sleaze of Kings Cross. *2 Roslyn St, Kings Cross, tel. 02/9356–4045. $5–$10. Tues.–Thurs. 7–3, Fri.–Sat. 8–5, Sun. 8–5.*

NIGHTCLUBS

BLACKMARKET NIGHTCLUB. Blackmarket opens its doors just as the other clubs are closing, revving up the music for night-shift workers and all-night party people until well past sunrise. On Thursday nights the club hosts Hellfire, Sydney's most prominent S & M club. *111 Regent St., Chippendale, tel. 02/9298–8863. $15. Thurs. 10 PM–3 AM, weekends 4 AM–11 AM.*

THE CAULDRON. This disco, with its accompanying quality restaurant near Kings Cross, is the place where Sydney's well-heeled sophisticates gather. Despite the name, the club is spacious and airy, except on weekends, when it's packed to the rafters. *207 Darlinghurst Rd., Darlinghurst, tel. 02/9331–1523. $10–$15. Tues.–Sat. 6–3.*

CLUB 77. This small basement club hosts a number of distinct scenes, each of which attracts a different crowd. Thursday night, "Kooky" draws the avant-garde, Friday is "Tweekin," a night of techno, Saturday is "Pure Pop," and Sunday is "Bazooka," featuring indie and alternative music and free entry. *77 William St., East Sydney, tel. 02/9361–4981. $5–$12. Thurs.–Sun. 9–3.*

DCM. Voted the best club in the southern hemisphere by *Harper's Bazaar* magazine, this remains Sydney's hottest dance club. "Dress to impress" is the code here, and minimalist Lycra apparel shows off the gym-hardened crowd to best advantage. The club is also popular with Sydney's gays. *31–33 Oxford St., Darlinghurst, tel. 02/9267–7380. $20. Thurs.–Fri. 11–7, Sat. 10 PM–10:30 AM, Sun. 9–7.*

ETTAMOGAH BAR AND FAMILY RESTAURANT. Based on a famous Australian cartoon series depicting an outback saloon, this theme pub has three bars and an open-air restaurant. The atmosphere varies from family-friendly during the day to nightclub in the evening. *225 Harbourside, Darling Harbour, tel. 02/9281–3922. Thurs.–Sat. $5–$10. Weekdays 11 AM–midnight, Sat. 11 AM–3 AM, Sun. 11 AM–11 PM.*

LIZARD LOUNGE. The Exchange Hotel's upstairs cocktail lounge/dance club offers a more refined alternative to the raucous action of the street-level bar. Specialty beers are served, as well as the latest cocktails. *34 Oxford St., Darlinghurst, tel. 02/9331–1936. $5 (Sat. only). Mon.–Thurs. 5–1, Fri.–Sun. 5–3.*

SOHO BAR. This is the grooviest and most civilized cocktail bar in Kings Cross, and the mood on the upper story is young, hip, and elegant. The dress code is smart, stylish, and strictly enforced. The adjoining pool room is rated one of the city's finest. *171 Victoria St., Potts Point, tel. 02/9358–6511. $10. Daily 6–3.*

PUBS WITH MUSIC

MERCANTILE HOTEL. In the shadow of Harbour Bridge, this hotel is Irish and very proud of it. Fiddles, drums, and pipes rise above the clamor in the bar, and lilting accents rejoice in song seven nights a week. *25 George St., the Rocks, tel. 02/9247–3570. Sun.–Wed. 10 AM–midnight, Thurs.–Sat. 10 AM–1 AM.*

ROSE, SHAMROCK AND THISTLE. Popularly known as the Three Weeds, this friendly, boisterous pub 5 km (3 mi) from the city center is one of the best places to hear live music, generally from Thursday through Saturday. *193 Evans St., Rozelle, tel. 02/9810–2244. Music nights $5–$10. Mon.–Sat. noon–midnight, Sun. noon–10.*

In This Chapter

The Rocks and Circular Quay 131 • City Center Area 137 • Paddington and Woollahra 138 • East of the City 138 • Sydney Area Lodging 140

Updated by Michael Gebicki

where to stay

SYDNEY HAS NUMEROUS accommodations options, from glamorous five-star hotels to bed & breakfast establishments, the latter of which can be found even close to the heart of the city. The best address in town is undoubtedly the Rocks, which combines harbor views and proximity to major cultural attractions, restaurants, shops, and galleries with a tranquil atmosphere. The area around Kings Cross is the city's second major hotel district. Visitors should remember, however, that this is also the city's major nightlife district, much of it unsavory in character.

If you arrive in Sydney without a hotel reservation, the best place to start looking is the **Tourism New South Wales information counter** at the international airport, which acts as a clearinghouse for hotel rooms. It can usually give you significant savings on published room rates.

CATEGORY	COST*
$$$$	over $300
$$$	$180–$300
$$	$135–$180
$	under $135

**All prices are for a standard double room.*

THE ROCKS AND CIRCULAR QUAY

$$$$ ANA HOTEL. Towering above Sydney Harbour from a prime position in the Rocks, this is Sydney's largest hotel and *the* place to go for a view. Rooms are opulent and decorated with a subdued Asian theme. Although the harbor views of the north-facing rooms are among the finest in town, views on the other sides—Darling Harbour, the city, or the eastern suburbs—are only marginally less impressive. On the 36th floor, the glass wall of the Horizons Bar provides the best views of Sydney Harbour, especially in the evening. *176 Cumberland St., 2000, tel. 02/9250–6000, fax 02/9250–6250. 548 rooms, 22 suites. 5 restaurants, 3 bars, in-room data ports, in-room safes, minibars, no-smoking rooms, room service, indoor pool, beauty salon, sauna, spa, exercise room, dry cleaning, laundry service, concierge, business services, convention center, meeting rooms, parking (fee). AE, DC, MC, V. www.anahotelsyd.com.au*

$$$$ HOTEL INTER-CONTINENTAL SYDNEY. This sleek, sophisticated, multistory hotel rises from the honey-colored sandstone facade of the historic Treasury Building, adding a note of warmth and tradition. It's also near the harbor and within easy walking distance of Circular Quay, the Opera House, and the central business district. The best views are from the rooms facing north, which overlook Harbour Bridge, or from the rooms on the eastern side of the hotel. Three executive floors offer valet and limousine service to and from the airport and complimentary breakfast and evening cocktails in the private lounges. *117 Macquarie St., 2000, tel. 02/9230–0200, fax 02/9240–1240. 465 rooms, 33 suites. 5 restaurants, bar, in-room safes, minibars, no-smoking rooms, room service, indoor pool, exercise room, dry cleaning, laundry service, concierge, business services, convention center, meeting rooms, parking (fee). AE, DC, MC, V. sydney.interconti.com/index.html*

$$$$ ★ OBSERVATORY HOTEL. Located in a quiet back street in the Rocks, this small, elegant hotel is a popular choice for those who prefer a less conspicuous city address. Throughout the hotel, antique reproductions accented by Venetian and Asian mementos create a warm, opulent character that evokes the mood of a gracious Georgian country house. Guest rooms are extremely spacious and decorated in a restrained color scheme with quality fabrics and walnut furnishings. The best are the junior suites, in particular rooms 313 and 310. The health club is the finest of any city hotel. The four-story hotel's single weakness is its lack of views. *89–113 Kent St., 2000, tel. 02/9256–2222, fax 02/9256–2233. 78 rooms, 22 suites. 2 restaurants, bar, in-room data ports, in-room safes, in-room VCRs, minibars, no-smoking floor, room service, indoor pool, sauna, steam room, exercise room, health club, dry cleaning, laundry service, concierge, business services, convention center, meeting rooms, parking (fee).* AE, DC, MC, V. *www.observatoryhotel.orient-express.com/index.html*

$$$$ ★ PARK HYATT SYDNEY. Moored in the shadow of Harbour Bridge, this is the city's most expensive hotel, with the finest location of any in Sydney. Its character is luxurious, cosmopolitan, and distinguished by the extra dash of sophistication (such as butler service) that is the hallmark of Park Hyatts. The color scheme is dominated by sandstone and earth tones, and the decor combines reproductions of classical statuary with contemporary bronzes and Australian artwork. Most rooms in the four-story hotel overlook Campbell's Cove and the Opera House. Most also have balconies. Don't miss the excellent fine-dining experience at the newly remodeled harbourkitchen & bar (☞ Rocks and Circular Quay in Eating Out). *7 Hickson Rd., 2000, tel. 02/9241–1234, fax 02/9256–1555. 122 rooms, 36 suites. 2 restaurants, bar, in-room data ports, minibars, no-smoking rooms, room service, indoor pool, beauty salon, sauna, spa, exercise room, dry cleaning, laundry service, concierge, business services, convention center, meeting rooms, parking (fee).* AE, DC, MC, V. *sydney.hyatt.com/sydph*

$$$$ ★ REGENT OF SYDNEY. Opened in 1983, this harbor-front hotel closed for several months in 1999 for a total makeover, and has emerged with a fresher, glossier look. The hotel is aimed at corporate clients and well-heeled vacationers, and the rooms, location, facilities, and service make this a top choice among Sydney's international-style hotels. Rooms are luxurious, and about half have unobstructed views of the Opera House and Harbour Bridge. Executive suites are especially large, and a reasonable value at around $500 per night. *199 George St., 2000, tel. 02/9238–0000, fax 02/9251–2851. 528 rooms, 66 suites. 4 restaurants, 2 bars, in-room safes,*

central sydney lodging

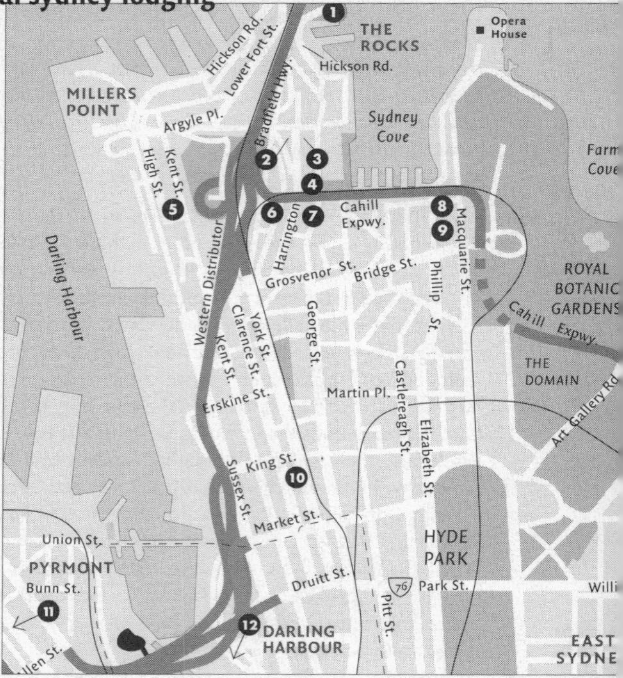

ANA Hotel, 6
Brooklyn Bed and Breakfast, 12
Double Bay Bed and Breakfast, 18
The Grace Hotel, 10
Harbour Rocks Hotel, 3
Hotel Inter-Continental Sydney, 9
The Hughenden, 19
Medusa, 13
Observatory Hotel, 5
Park Hyatt Sydney, 1
Ravesi's on Bondi Beach, 20
Regent of Sydney, 7
Ritz-Carlton, Sydney, 8
The Russell, 4
Sebel of Sydney, 17

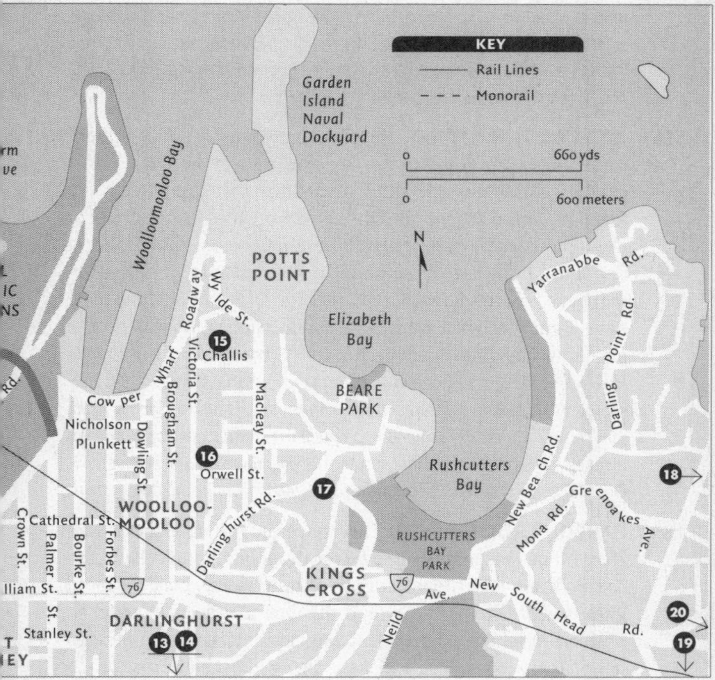

Simpsons of Potts Point, **15**

Stafford Apartments Sydney, **2**

Sullivans Hotel, **14**

Trickett's, **11**

Victoria Court Sydney, **16**

minibars, no-smoking rooms, room service, pool, beauty salon, massage, sauna, steam room, exercise room, dry cleaning, laundry service, concierge, business services, convention center, meeting rooms, parking (fee). AE, DC, MC, V. www.regenthotels.com/hotels/sydney

$$$$ ★ RITZ-CARLTON, SYDNEY. This small, unobtrusive establishment is the most sumptuous of the city's deluxe elite hotels. It is in a prime position close to the Opera House, Circular Quay, the Royal Botanic Gardens, and the central business district. Decor throughout is a mixture of marble, antiques, warm-toned fabrics, and soft lighting—an intimate and opulent blend that evokes the European hotel tradition. Rooms are large and luxurious, and most have French doors leading to a small balcony. Rooms on the east side have views of the Botanic Gardens and the Opera House. *93 Macquarie St., 2000, tel. 02/9252–4600, fax 02/9252–4286. 94 rooms, 12 suites. Restaurant, bar, minibars, no-smoking rooms, room service, pool, sauna, exercise room, dry cleaning, laundry service, concierge, business services, convention center, meeting rooms, parking (fee). AE, DC, MC, V. www.ritzcarlton.com/location/Australia/Sydney/main.htm*

$$$ HARBOUR ROCKS HOTEL. This converted, historic Rocks wool store offers reasonable value for location, but limited character. Top-floor rooms on the eastern side of the four-story building afford glimpses of Circular Quay and the Opera House. In order to preserve the character of the building, the hotel is air-conditioned only in the public areas, and there are no guest elevators. *34–52 Harrington St., 2000, tel. 02/9251–8944, fax 02/9251–8900. 55 rooms. Restaurant, bar, in-room safes, minibars, laundry service. AE, DC, MC, V.*

$$$ STAFFORD APARTMENTS SYDNEY. Located in a premium position in the Rocks, this establishment has self-contained apartments as well as hotel rooms with kitchen facilities, making it a good choice for anyone looking for longer-term accommodation. Decor and furnishings are tasteful but spare, with a Scandinavian feel that is both elegant and uncluttered. Rooms on the fourth through sixth floors of the main building have views across Circular Quay to the

Opera House. *75 Harrington St., 2000, tel. 02/9251–6711, fax 02/9251–3458. 54 apartments. In-room data ports, in-room safes, pool, sauna, spa, exercise room, dry cleaning, laundry service, business services, parking (fee). AE, DC, MC, V.*

$$ ★ THE RUSSELL. For charm, character, and central location, it would be hard to beat this small, century-old hotel on the edge of the Rocks. No two rooms are quite the same, and rates vary considerably depending on room size and facilities. The spacious double rooms at the front have views of Circular Quay. There are also somewhat quieter, standard-size double rooms overlooking Nurses Walk or opening onto an internal courtyard. In keeping with the Victorian character of the hotel, rooms are not air-conditioned, but all have ceiling fans and windows that open. Breakfast is included. *143A George St., 2000, tel. 02/9241–3543, fax 02/9252–1652. 29 rooms. Restaurant. AE, DC, MC, V.*

CITY CENTER AREA

$$$ THE GRACE HOTEL. At the heart of the city's shopping and business district, this hotel opened after a total restoration in 1997, retaining traces of the art-deco style of its origins. Rooms are well-proportioned, uncluttered, and furnished in warm, soothing colors. The hotel is especially popular with corporate travelers. During World War II, the building was used as the Sydney headquarters for General Douglas MacArthur's Pacific campaign. Despite the busy location, rooms are quiet. Those that overlook the central well of the building are recommended for jet-lagged travelers in search of total silence. *77 York St., 2000, tel. 02/9272–6888, fax 02/9229–8189. 382 rooms, 6 suites. 2 restaurants, bar, in-room data ports, in-room safes, no-smoking floors, room service, indoor lap pool, sauna, spa, steam room, exercise room, laundry service, dry cleaning, business services, convention center, meeting rooms. AE, DC, MC, V. www.gracehotel.com.au*

PADDINGTON AND WOOLLAHRA

$$ **THE HUGHENDEN.** This Victorian mansion was recently converted to accommodate travelers at a prestigious eastern-suburbs address. Rooms are small but prettily decorated, and each has an en suite bathroom. Rooms 21, 23, 24, and 25 are the largest, although they overlook the moderately busy street below. Near many of Sydney's finest antiques shops and art dealers, the hotel offers easy access to Oxford Street, Centennial Park, and Paddington. The city and the eastern beaches are 10–15 minutes by public transport. Smoking is not permitted in guest rooms. A full breakfast is included. *14 Queen St., Woollahra 2025, tel. 02/9363–4863, fax 02/9362–0398. 36 rooms. Restaurant, bar, library. AE, DC, MC, V.*

$ **SULLIVANS HOTEL.** This small, friendly, family-owned and -operated hotel is an exceptional value. Just a 15-minute walk from the city in fashionable Paddington, the hotel is close to the shops, cafés, restaurants, movie theaters, and nightlife of Oxford Street. The best rooms are those overlooking the central courtyard, pool, and the terrace houses at the rear. Those that overlook the city are more likely to be affected by traffic noise. Bathrooms and desks in most rooms were upgraded in 1998. *21 Oxford St., Paddington 2021, tel. 02/9361–0211, fax 02/9360–3735. 62 rooms. Breakfast room, pool, bicycles. AE, DC, MC, V.*

EAST OF THE CITY

$$$$ **SEBEL OF SYDNEY.** Situated close to the Kings Cross nightlife district, this hotel makes the most of its reputation as the favorite of visiting music and movie stars of the 1960s and 70s. The atmosphere remains friendly and clublike, although visiting celebs usually choose one of Sydney's more glamorous waterfront hotels these days. Rooms are spacious and well equipped, and they are often available at a considerable discount now that fashion has passed the hotel by. Views aren't a notable feature, although those that face east above the seventh-floor overlook the yacht basin in Rushcutters Bay. *23 Elizabeth Bay Rd., Elizabeth Bay 2011, tel.*

02/9358–3244, fax 02/9357–1926. 140 rooms, 26 suites. Restaurant, bar, no-smoking rooms, room service, pool, sauna, exercise room, dry cleaning, laundry service, concierge, business services, convention center, meeting rooms. AE, DC, MC, V.

$$$ MEDUSA. Housed inside a Victorian terrace house, this small, elegant establishment has broken new ground among Sydney's hotels, and the international style arbiters have applauded long and loud. In fact, *Conde Nast Traveler* magazine named this one of the 21 "coolest" hotels for the 21st century, the only Australian Hotel to make the list. The staff is dressed by Armani, colors are brash, and furnishings might have come direct from a Milan design gallery. Every room is different, and each features a kitchenette. Behind the glamour is a comfortable, well-run hotel with friendly, attentive staff and exceptional accommodation at this price level. *267 Darlinghurst Rd., Darlinghurst 2010, tel. 02/9331–1000, fax 02/9380–6901. 18 rooms. Bar, in-room data ports, kitchenettes, minibars. AE, DC, MC, V.*

$$$ SIMPSONS OF POTTS POINT. On a quiet street just a few minutes' stroll from Kings Cross, this hotel retains many decorative features from its Victorian origins, including stained-glass windows and a grand cedar staircase. Rooms are comfortable and decorated in a modestly opulent period style. The best is the slightly more expensive Cloud Room, which has a palatial en suite bathroom. Continental breakfast is included. Guests who book via the Internet receive a 10% discount. *8 Challis Ave., Potts Point 2011, tel. 02/9356–2199, fax 02/9356–4476. 14 rooms. Breakfast room, free parking. AE, DC, MC, V. www.simpsonspottspoint.com.au*

$$ DOUBLE BAY BED AND BREAKFAST. In one of Sydney's most exclusive harborside suburbs, this two-story terrace house run by the affable Bill and Margaret Cox offers a high standard of comfort at an affordable price. The house is richly decorated with antiques, and all of the soft furnishings are made by Margaret, who has a background in fashion. Breakfast is the full monty: eggs Benedict, homemade breads, smoked salmon, crepes with ricotta, and for traditional types, steak, bacon, tomatoes, and eggs. *63 Cross St., Double Bay 2028, tel. 02/9363–4776, fax 02/9363–1992. 3 rooms, 2 with bath. Breakfast room, free parking. AE, DC, MC, V. www.ozemail.com.au/doubaybb*

$$ VICTORIA COURT SYDNEY. Set on a leafy street near Kings Cross, this small, smart hotel is appealing for more than just its reasonable rates. Hand-painted tiles and etched-glass doors recall its Victorian ancestry, yet the rooms come with the modern blessings of en suite bathrooms and comfortable beds. *122 Victoria St., Potts Point 2011, tel. 02/9357–3200, fax 02/9357–7606. 25 rooms. Breakfast room. AE, DC, MC, V.*

SYDNEY AREA LODGING

$$ RAVESI'S ON BONDI BEACH. This small boutique hotel looks out on Australia's most famous beach and offers a dash of style at a moderate price. All rooms are spacious, well kept, and uncluttered, decorated in a stylish sand-and-sea color scheme enhanced by art-deco touches, in keeping with the building's origins. Oceanfront rooms have the best views, in particular Room 6. For family-size space, the split-level suites, which have their own terrace, are recommended. Least expensive are those double rooms without a sea view. The second-floor restaurant is popular and noisy. Request a room on the top floor for peace and privacy. Frequent bus service takes 25 minutes to get to the city. *Campbell Parade and Hall St., Bondi Beach 2026, tel. 02/9365–4422, fax 02/9365–1481. 16 rooms. Restaurant, bar. AE, DC, MC, V.*

$$ TRICKETT'S. A quiet location in a historic suburb, easy access to the city, and great value make this one of the picks of Sydney's bed-and-breakfast accommodations. The Victorian character of this converted mansion is evident in the 13-ft ceilings, the ballroom, and the hallways elegantly enhanced with Oriental rugs and porcelain. Guest rooms are vast and simply furnished, and each has a bathroom with robes supplied. There are many dining options within walking distance, and a spacious waterfront park at the bottom of the street. Continental breakfast is included. 270 *Glebe Point Rd., Glebe 2037, tel. 02/9552–1141, fax 02/9692–9462. 7 rooms. Breakfast room, free parking. No credit cards.*

$ **BROOKLYN BED & BREAKFAST.** Tucked away in an inner-west suburb, this late-Victorian guest house offers accommodations with character and exceptional value. Bedrooms are on the upper level, and except for the single room at the rear, all are large and comfortable and equipped to sleep three. The front room with balcony is especially recommended. The house is a 15-minute train ride from the city. The cafés and restaurants of Norton Street, Sydney's "little Italy," are within a 10-minute walk. Owner Angela Finnigan is convivial and helpful. 25 *Railway St., Petersham 2049, tel. 02/9564–2312. 5 rooms. Breakfast room, free parking. AE, DC, MC, V.*

PRACTICAL INFORMATION

Air Travel

Flights to Sydney leave from Los Angeles, Honolulu, New York, Toronto, and Vancouver, as well as from London, Frankfurt, and Rome. Depending on your airline and route, you can elect to stop over in Honolulu, Fiji, Tahiti, or Auckland from the U.S.; and Singapore, Colombo, the United Arab Emirates, Mauritius, Johannesburg, Mumbai, or Bangkok from Europe. Nonstop service is available to Sydney from Los Angeles.

BOOKING

When you book **look for nonstop flights** and **remember that "direct" flights stop at least once.** Try to avoid connecting flights, which require a change of plane.

CARRIERS

Now that it's no longer government owned, Australia's Qantas (and its domestic subsidiaries such as Eastern Australia, Southern Australia, Sunstate, and Airlink) is considered the national carrier, the other one being Ansett (and its regional subsidiaries, such as Kendell), which also operates an international service. Air Kangaroo Island and Airlines of South Australia serve the country's southern regions.

➤ **To and From Australia: Air New Zealand** (tel. 800/262–1234 in the U.S.; 800/663–5494 in Canada; 020/8741–2299 in the U.K.; 13–2476 or 02/8904–8800 in Australia; 0800/737000 in New Zealand). **British Airways** (tel. 800/247–9297 in the U.S. and Canada; 0345/222111 in the U.K.; 09/366–3200 in New Zealand). **Air Canada** (tel. 800/426–7000 in the U.S.; 800/665–1177 in Canada; 09/379–3371 in New Zealand). **Cathay Pacific** (tel. 800/233–2742 in the U.S.; 800/268–6868 in Canada; 020/7747–8888 in the U.K.; 13–1747 in Australia; 09/379–0861 in New Zealand). **Japan Airlines** (tel. 800/525–3663 in the U.S.; 800/525–3663 in Canada; 02/9272–1111 in Australia; 020/7408–1000 in the U.K.; 09/379–3202 in New Zealand). **Qantas** (tel. 800/227–4500 in the U.S.; 800/227–4500 in Canada; 0800/747767 in the U.K.; 13–1313 in Australia; 09/357–8900 in New Zealand). **Singapore Airlines** (tel. 800/742–3333 in the U.S.; 800/387–0038 in Canada; 020/8747–0007 in the U.K.; 13–1011 in Australia; 03/374–7100 in New Zealand). **United** (tel. 800/538–2929 in the U.S; 800/241–6522 in Canada; 0845/844–4777 in the U.K.; 13–1777 in Australia; 09/379–3800 in New Zealand).

➤ WITHIN AUSTRALIA: **Air Kangaroo Island** (tel. 13–1301). **Airlines of South Australia** (tel. 08/8234–3000). **Ansett** (tel. 800/366–1300 in the U.S. and Canada; 020/7434–4071 in the U.K.; 13–1300 in Australia). **Kendell** (tel. 13–1300 in Australia). **Qantas** (tel. 13–1713; 13–1313 in Australia).

FLYING TIMES

Flying times from New York to Sydney (via Los Angeles) are about 21 hours; from Chicago to Sydney (via Los Angeles) about 19 hours; from Los Angeles to Sydney (nonstop) about 15 hours; from Los Angeles to Melbourne (via Auckland) around 16 hours; and from London to Sydney or Melbourne about 20½ hours via Singapore or Bangkok.

Airports & Transfers

Kingsford–Smith is Sydney's main airport, 8 km (5 mi) south of the city. Trolleys are available in the baggage area of the international terminal. You can convert your money to Australian currency at the Thomas Cook bureaus, in both the arrivals and departures areas, open from about 5 AM to 10 PM or later, depending on flight arrival or departure times.

Tourism New South Wales has two information counters in the international terminal's arrivals hall. One provides free maps and brochures and handles general inquiries. The other deals with accommodations bookings. Both counters are open daily from approximately 6 AM to 11 PM.

Kingsford–Smith's domestic and international terminals are 3 km (2 mi) apart. To get from one terminal to the other, you can take a taxi for about $11, use the Airport Shuttle Bus, or catch the Airport Express bus. The latter departs approximately every 10–15 minutes, between about 5 AM and 11 PM, and both cost $2.50.

The green-and-yellow Airport Express bus provides a fast, comfortable link between the airport terminals and the city, Kings Cross, Bondi, Coogee, Darling Harbour, and Glebe. Buses depart at intervals of between 8 and 30 minutes from the airport, generally from around 6 AM to 11 PM. Refer to timetables outside the airport terminals for full details, or call the State Transit Infoline (tel. 13–1500). A brochure on the service is usually available from the Tourism New South Wales counter at the airport. Tickets are $6.50 for one-way and $11 round-trip.

Taxis are available from the ranks outside the terminal buildings. The fare to city hotels is about $30, about $28 to Kings Cross.

The Airport Link is a rail service that provides the shortest travel time between the city and the airport. The link meshes with the suburban rail network at Central Station and Circular Quay Station. The one-way fare is $8.

➤ AIRPORT INFORMATION: **Sydney Kingsford-Smith Airport** (tel. 02/9667–9111).

Boat & Ferry Travel

No finer introduction to the city is to be found than aboard one of the commuter ferries that ply Sydney Harbour. The hub of the ferry system is Circular Quay, and ferries run to almost 30 spots the length and breadth of the harbor between about 6 AM and 11:30 PM. The one-way Manly ferry fare is $4.60. Fares for shorter inner-harbor journeys start at $3.70. You can also buy economical ferry-and-entrance-fee passes, available from the Circular Quay ticket office, to such attractions as Taronga Zoo and Sydney Aquarium.

A fun, fast, but somewhat expensive way to get around is by water taxi. These operate to and from practically anywhere on Sydney Harbour that has wharf or steps access. Contact Harbour Taxi Boats or Taxis Afloat for details and bookings.

➤ **WATER TAXIS: Harbour Taxi Boats** (tel. 02/9555–1155). **Taxis Afloat** (tel. 02/9955–3222).

Bus Travel

On Sydney's well-developed bus system, fares are calculated by the number of city sections traveled. The minimum two-section bus fare ($1.50) applies to trips throughout the inner-city area. You would pay the minimum fare, for example, for a ride from Circular Quay to Kings Cross, or from Park Street to Oxford Street in Paddington. Tickets may be purchased from the driver. Discounted fares are available in several forms, including Travelten passes (valid for 10 journeys), which start at $8.80 and are available from bus stations and most newsagents.

A Travelpass allows you unlimited travel aboard buses, ferries, and trains, but not trams, within designated areas of the city for a week or more. The most useful is probably the weeklong Blue Travelpass ($20.00), which covers the city and eastern suburbs and inner-harbor ferries. (Ferries to Manly will cost extra.) Travelpasses are available from railway and bus stations and from most newsagents on bus routes.

If you're planning on spending three days or less in Sydney and taking the Airport Express bus, the guided Sydney Explorer and Bondi & Bay Explorer buses (☞ Tours and Packages, *below*), and any of the three sightseeing cruises operated by the State Transit Authority, Sydneypass ($85 for three days, five- and seven-day passes available) will save you money. The pass also allows unlimited travel on any public bus or harbor ferry and on most suburban train services. Purchase passes from the Tourism New South Wales counter on the ground floor of the international airport terminal or from the driver of any Explorer or Airport Express bus.

For route, timetable, and ticket price information on Sydney's buses, ferries, and trains call the State Transit Infoline.

➤ **Bus Information: State Transit Infoline** (tel. 13–1500, daily 6 AM–10 PM).

Business Hours

As a rule, business hours in Australia are weekdays 9–5. This applies to post offices as well. Banks are open Monday–Thursday 9:30–4, Friday 9:30–5. In some states a few banks are open on Saturday mornings. Most museums and major sights are open 7 days, including public holidays. Outside metropolitan areas, opening hours for museums and sights may vary considerably. Visitors are advised to check in advance. Pharmacies are open normally open weekdays 9–5:30, Sat. 9–12:30.

Car Rental

Rates in Sydney begin at $24 a day and $168 a week for an economy car with air-conditioning, manual transmission, and 100 free kilometers. This does not include tax on car rentals, which is 10%. Larger agencies such as Avis, Budget, Hertz, and Thrifty are the most likely to have rental desks located at airport terminals. Discount operators offer vehicles at about the same rate in major cities. Travelers renting a car in Sydney must purchase mandatory collision insurance, which is included in the price.

Renters are generally prohibited from driving non-four-wheel-drive rental vehicles on unsealed roads. If you do and you have a collision, you may find that insurance will not cover the damage.

➤ **Major Agencies: Alamo** (tel. 800/522–9696; 020/8759–6200 in the U.K.). **Avis** (tel. 800/331–1084; 800/331–1084 in Canada; 02/9353–9000 in Australia; 09/525–1982 in New Zealand). **Budget** (tel. 800/527–0700;0870/607–5000 in the U.K., through affiliate

Europcar). **Dollar** (tel. 800/800–6000; 0124/622–0111 in the U.K., through affiliate Sixt Kenning; 02/9223–1444 in Australia). **Hertz** (tel. 800/654–3001; 800/263–0600 in Canada; 020/8897–2072 in the U.K.; 02/9669–2444 in Australia; 09/256–8690 in New Zealand) **National Car Rental** (tel. 800/227–7368; 020/8680–4800 in the U.K., where it is known as National Europe).

INSURANCE

When driving a rented car you are generally responsible for any damage to or loss of the vehicle as well as for any property damage or personal injury that you may cause. Before you rent see what coverage your personal auto-insurance policy and credit cards already provide.

Although insurance is included with standard rental vehicles in Australia, you are still responsible for an "excess" fee—a maximum amount that you will have to pay if damage occurs. Fines can be incurred for such accidents as a cracked windshield, which is common occurrence on Australian roads. The amount of this "excess" is generally between $500 and $1,000, but you can have this figure reduced by paying a daily fee.

REQUIREMENTS & RESTRICTIONS

In Australia your own driver's license is accepted at some rental companies. An International Driver's Permit is required at others. It's available from the American or Canadian automobile association, and in the United Kingdom, from the Automobile Association or Royal Automobile Club. These international permits are universally recognized, and having one in your wallet may save you a problem with the local authorities.

In Australia you must be 21 to rent a car, and rates may be higher if you're under 25. There is no upper age limit for rental.

Car Travel

Driving is easy in Australia, once you adjust to traveling on the left. The catch phrase is: **Drive left, look right.** "Look right" is the pedestrian's caveat; for Americans, stepping into the street means looking left for oncoming traffic. Do that Down Under and you could be in trouble.

Speed limits are 50–60 kilometers per hour (kph) in populated areas, and 100–110 kph on open roads—the equivalent of 31–37 and 62–68 mph, respectively. Surveillance of speeders and "drink-driving" (the legal limit is a tough.05% blood-alcohol level) is thorough and penalties are high. Seat belts are mandatory nationwide for drivers and all passengers. Children must be restrained in a seat appropriate to their size. These can be rented from car-rental agencies.

EMERGENCY SERVICES

If you have an emergency requiring an ambulance, the fire department, or the police, dial 000. Many major highways now have telephones for breakdown assistance.

Each state has its own motoring organization that provides assistance for vehicle breakdowns. When you hire a vehicle, you are entitled to assistance from the relevant motoring organization, free of charge. A toll-free, nationwide number is available for roadside assistance.

➤ CONTACTS: **Motoring Organization Hotline** (tel. 13–1111).

GASOLINE

The cost of gasoline ("petrol") is about 78¢ per liter in Sydney. American Express, MasterCard, and Visa are accepted at most service stations. Pumps will be familiar to most drivers from North America and Europe.

Customs & Duties

When shopping, **keep receipts** for all purchases. Upon reentering the country, **be ready to show customs officials what you've bought.** If you feel a duty is incorrect or object to the way your clearance was handled, note the inspector's badge number and ask to see a supervisor. If the problem isn't resolved, write to the appropriate authorities, beginning with the port director at your point of entry.

IN AUSTRALIA

Australia has strict laws prohibiting or restricting the import of weapons and firearms. Antidrug laws are strictly enforced, and penalties are severe. All animals are subject to quarantine. Most canned or preserved food may be imported, but fresh fruit, vegetables, and all food served on board aircraft coming from other countries is forbidden. All food must be declared on your customs statement. Nonresidents over 18 years of age may bring in 250 cigarettes, or 250 grams of cigars or tobacco, and 1.125 liters of liquor, provided this is carried with them. Other taxable goods to the value of A$400 for adults and A$200 for children may be included in personal baggage duty-free.

Australian Customs Service (Regional Director, Box 8, Sydney, NSW 2001, tel. 1300–363–263, fax 02/9213–4000).

IN CANADA

Canadian residents who have been out of Canada for at least 7 days may bring home C$500 worth of goods duty-free. If you've been away less than 7 days but more than 48 hours, the duty-free allowance drops to C$200. If your trip lasts 24–48 hours, the allowance is C$50. You may not pool allowances with family members. Goods claimed under the C$500 exemption may follow you by mail. Those claimed under the lesser exemptions must accompany you. Alcohol and tobacco products may be included in the 7-day and 48-hour exemptions but not in the 24-hour exemption. If you meet the age requirements of the province or territory through which you reenter Canada, you may bring in, duty-free, 1.14 liters (40 imperial ounces) of wine or liquor *or* 24 12-ounce cans or bottles of beer or ale. If you are 16 or older you may bring in, duty-free, 200 cigarettes and 50 cigars. Check ahead of time with Revenue Canada or the Department of Agriculture for policies regarding meat products, seeds, plants, and fruits.

You may send an unlimited number of gifts worth up to C$60 each duty-free to Canada. Label the package UNSOLICITED GIFT—VALUE UNDER $60. Alcohol and tobacco are excluded.

➤ **INFORMATION: Revenue Canada** (2265 St. Laurent Blvd. S, Ottawa, Ontario K1G 4K3, tel. 613/993–0534; 800/461–9999 in Canada, fax 613/957–8911, www.ccra-adrc.gc.ca).

IN NEW ZEALAND

Homeward-bound residents 17 or older may bring back $700 worth of souvenirs and gifts. Your duty-free allowance also includes 4.5 liters of wine or beer; one 1,125-ml bottle of spirits; and either 200 cigarettes, 250 grams of tobacco, 50 cigars, or a combination of the three up to 250 grams. Prohibited items include meat products, seeds, plants, and fruits.

➤ **INFORMATION: New Zealand Customs** (Custom House, 50 Anzac Ave., Box 29, Auckland, New Zealand, tel. 09/359–6655, fax 09/359–6732).

IN THE U.K.

From countries outside the EU, including Australia, you may bring home, duty-free, 200 cigarettes or 50 cigars; 1 liter of spirits or 2 liters of fortified or sparkling wine or liqueurs; 2 liters of still table wine; 60 ml of perfume; 250 ml of toilet water; plus £136 worth of other goods, including gifts and souvenirs. If returning from outside the EU, prohibited items include meat products, seeds, plants, and fruits.

➤ **INFORMATION: HM Customs and Excise** (Dorset House, Stamford St., Bromley, Kent BR1 1XX, tel. 020/7202–4227).

IN THE U.S.

U.S. residents who have been out of the country for at least 48 hours (and who have not used the $400 allowance or any part of it in the past 30 days) may bring home $400 worth of foreign goods duty-free. U.S. residents 21 and older may bring back 1 liter of alcohol duty-free. In addition, regardless of your age, you are allowed 200 cigarettes and 100 non-Cuban cigars. Antiques, which the U.S. Customs Service defines as objects more than 100 years old, enter duty-free, as do original works of art done entirely by hand, including paintings, drawings, and sculptures.

You may also send packages home duty-free: up to $200 worth of goods for personal use, with a limit of one parcel per addressee per day (except alcohol or tobacco products or perfume worth more than $5). Label the package PERSONAL USE and attach a list of its contents and their retail value. Do not label the package UNSOLICITED GIFT or your duty-free exemption will drop to $100. Mailed items do not affect your duty-free allowance on your return.

➤ **INFORMATION: U.S. Customs Service** (1300 Pennsylvania Ave. NW, Washington, DC 20229, www.customs.gov; inquiries tel. 202/354–1000; complaints c/o Office of Regulations and Rulings; registration of equipment c/o Resource Management, tel. 202/927–0540).

Dining

Some Australian restaurants offer a fixed-price dinner, but the majority are à la carte. It's wise to **make a reservation** and **inquire if the restaurant has a liquor license** or is "BYOB" or "BYO" (Bring Your Own Bottle).

Down Under, entrée means appetizer and main courses are American entrées. "Bistro" generally refers to a relatively inexpensive place. French fries are called chips. If you want ketchup, ask for tomato sauce.

The restaurants we list are the cream of the crop in each price category.

MEALTIMES

Breakfast is usually served 7–10, lunch 11:30–2:30, and dinner service begins around 6:30. In the cities, a variety of dining options are available at all hours. The choices are far more restricted in the countryside.

Unless otherwise noted, the restaurants listed in this guide are open daily for lunch and dinner.

RESERVATIONS & DRESS

Reservations are always a good idea. We mention them only when they're essential or not accepted. Book as far ahead as you can, and reconfirm as soon as you arrive. We mention dress only when men are required to wear a jacket or a jacket and tie.

Discounts & Deals

Be a smart shopper and **compare all your options** before making decisions. A plane ticket bought with a promotional coupon from travel clubs, coupon books, and direct-mail offers may not be cheaper than the least expensive fare from a discount ticket agency. And always keep in mind that what you get is just as important as what you save.

Electricity

To use your U.S.-purchased electric-powered equipment, **bring a converter and adapter.** The electrical current in Australia is 240 volts, 50 cycles alternating current (AC). Wall outlets take slanted three-prong plugs (but not the U.K. three-prong) and plugs with two flat prongs set in a V.

If your appliances are dual-voltage, you'll need only an adapter. Don't use 110-volt outlets, marked FOR SHAVERS ONLY, for high-wattage appliances such as blow-dryers. Most laptops operate equally well on 110 and 220 volts and so require only an adapter.

Embassies and Consulates

➤ **CANADA: Canadian Embassy** (Level 5, Quay West 111, Harrington St., Sydney, tel. 61/2364–3050).

➤ **NEW ZEALAND: New Zealand High Commission** (Commonwealth Ave., Canberra, tel. 61/6270–4211).

➤ **UNITED KINGDOM: British Consulate General** (Gateway Bldg., 1 Macquarie Pl., Level 16, Sydney Cove, tel. 02/9247–7521).

➤ **UNITED STATES: U.S. Consulate General** (MLC Centre, Level 59, 19–29 Martin Place, Sydney, tel. 02/9373–9200).

Emergencies

➤ **CONTACTS: Fire, police, or ambulance:** tel. 000. **Dental Emergency Information Service:** tel. 02/9369–7050, after 7 PM daily. **Hospitals:** Royal North Shore Hospital (Pacific Hwy., St. Leonards, tel. 02/9926–7111); St. Vincent's Public Hospital (Victoria and Burton Sts., Darlinghurst, tel. 02/9339–1111). **Police (nonemergency):** Sydney Police Centre (tel. 02/9281–0000).

Health

Hygiene standards in Australia are high and well monitored, so **don't worry about drinking the water or eating fresh produce.** The primary health hazard is sunburn or sunstroke; even people who are not normally bothered by strong sun should cover up with a long-sleeve shirt, a hat, and long pants or a beach wrap. Keep in mind that at higher altitudes you will burn more easily. **Apply sunscreen liberally** before you go out—even for a half hour—and wear a visored cap and sunglasses. Dehydration is a serious danger that can be easily avoided, so be sure to carry water and drink often.

You may take a four weeks' supply of prescribed medication into Australia (more with a doctor's certificate). Your best bet for a late-night pharmacy is in the major city hotels or in the Kings Cross and Oxford Street (Darlinghurst) areas. You can also call the Pharmacy Guild 24 hours a day for advice and assistance (tel. 02/9235–0333).

DIVERS' ALERT

Do not fly within 24 hours of scuba diving.

MEDICAL PLANS

No one plans to get sick while traveling, but it happens, so **consider signing up with a medical-assistance company.** Members get doctor referrals, emergency evacuation or repatriation, hot lines for medical consultation, cash for emergencies, and other assistance.

➤ MEDICAL-ASSISTANCE COMPANIES: **International SOS Assistance** (8 Neshaminy Interplex, Suite 207, Trevose, PA 19053, tel. 215/245–4707 or 800/523–6586, fax 215/244–9617, www.internationalsos.com; 12 Chemin Riantbosson, 1217 Meyrin 1, Geneva, Switzerland, tel. 4122/785–6464, fax 4122/785–6424, www.internationalsos.com).

Language

To an outsider's ear, Australian English can be mystifying. Not only is the accent thick and slightly slurred, but Australians have developed a vibrant vernacular quite distinct from that of any other English-speaking country. You can soon learn the idiom and how to speak "strine"—as Aussies (who also call themselves "Ozzies") pronounce "Australian"—with a copy of Danielle Martin's *Australians Say G'Day*, which comes with a cassette-tape recording to help you interpret the book's dialogues. Other useful guides to the intricacies of Australian terminology are *Australian Slang*, by Lenie Johansen, and *The Best of Aussie Slang*, by John Blackman.

Lodging

The lodgings we list are the cream of the crop in each price category. We always list the facilities that are available, but we don't specify whether they cost extra. When pricing accommodations, always ask what's included and what costs extra. Properties indicated by an are lodging establishments whose restaurant warrants a special trip.

Assume that hotels operate on the **European Plan** (EP, with no meals) unless we specify that they use either the **Continental Plan** (CP, with a Continental breakfast) or the **Modified American Plan** or are **all-inclusive** (including all meals and most activities). Surcharges sometimes apply on weekends, long weekends, and during holiday seasons.

Mail & Shipping

Allow a week for letters and postcards to reach the United States and the U.K. Letters to New Zealand generally take 4–5 days. All mail travels by air.

OVERNIGHT SERVICES

Both DHL and Federal Express operate fast, reliable express courier services from Australia. Rates are around $45 for a 2-pound (1-kilo) parcel to the U.S. or Europe, including door-to-door service. Delivery time between Sydney and New York is approximately three days.

➤ **MAJOR SERVICES: DHL Worldwide Express,** (tel. 13–1406). **Fedex,** (tel. 13–2610).

POSTAL RATES

Mail service in Australia is normally efficient. Postage rates are $1.05 per 20-gram (28.35 grams = 1 ounce) airmail letter and 95¢ for airmail postcards to North America. The same airmail services cost $1.20 and $1 to the United Kingdom. Overseas fax service costs around $10 for the first page plus $4 for each additional page. You can send printed material by Economy Air, which travels via surface mail within Australia but by airmail across the Pacific, at a cost of $19 for up to a kilogram (a little more than 2 pounds).

Money Matters

Prices for goods and services can be volatile. Still those cited below may be used as an approximate guide, since variation should rarely exceed 10%.

Prices throughout this guide are given for adults. Substantially reduced fees are almost always available for children, students, and senior citizens. For information on taxes, *see* Taxes, *below*.

ATMS

Most suburban shopping centers and malls have at least one nonbank ATM. The most widely accepted cards are Visa, MasterCard, and American Express. Those linked to the Cirrus network are also widely accepted at ATMs. Make sure your ATM card has a 4-digit PIN.

CREDIT CARDS

Throughout this guide, the following abbreviations are used: **AE,** American Express; **DC,** Diner's Club; **MC,** MasterCard; and **V,** Visa.

➤ **Reporting Lost Cards: American Express** (tel. 02/9271–8666). **MasterCard** (tel. 1800/12–0113). **Visa** (tel. 1800/805–341).

CURRENCY

All prices listed in this guide are quoted in Australian dollars. Australia's currency operates on a decimal system, with the dollar (A$) as the basic unit and 100 cents (¢) equaling $1. Bills come in $100, $50, $20, $10, and $5 denominations, which are differentiated by color and size. Coins are minted in $2, $1, 50¢, 20¢, 10¢, and 5¢ denominations.

CURRENCY EXCHANGE

At press time, the exchange rate was about A$1.68 to the U.S. dollar, $1.04 to the Canadian dollar, $2.70 to the pound sterling, and 84¢ to the New Zealand dollar.

For the most favorable rates, **change money through banks.** Although ATM transaction fees may be higher abroad than at home, ATM rates are excellent because they are based on wholesale rates offered only by major banks. To avoid lines at airport exchange booths, **get a bit of local currency before you leave home.**

➤ **Exchange Services: International Currency Express** (tel. 888/278–6628 for orders, www.foreignmoney.com). **Thomas Cook Currency Services** (tel. 800/287–7362 for telephone orders and retail locations, www.us.thomascook.com).

TRAVELER'S CHECKS

Lost or stolen checks can usually be replaced within 24 hours. To ensure a speedy refund, buy your own traveler's checks. Don't let someone else pay for them. Irregularities like this can cause delays. The person who bought the checks should make the call to request a refund.

Packing

In your carry-on luggage, **pack an extra pair of eyeglasses or contact lenses and enough of any medication** you take to last the entire trip. You may also ask your doctor to write a spare prescription using the drug's generic name, since brand names may vary from country to country. In luggage to be checked, **never pack prescription drugs or valuables.** To avoid customs delays, carry medications in their original packaging. And don't forget to carry with you the addresses of offices that handle refunds of lost traveler's checks.

Passports & Visas

When traveling internationally, **carry your passport even if you don't need one** (it's always the best form of I.D.) and **make two photocopies of the data page** (one for someone at home and another for you, carried separately from your passport). If you lose your passport, promptly call the nearest embassy or consulate and the local police.

ENTERING AUSTRALIA

All U.S. citizens, even infants, need a valid passport to enter Australia for stays of up to 90 days. A visa is also required.

Qantas passengers may obtain an Australian visa from that airline. Otherwise application forms are available from one of the offices listed below. Children traveling on a parent's passport do not need a separate application form, but should be included under Item 16 on the parent's form.

Visitors planning to stay more than three months must pay a fee. Check with the Consulate-General to ascertain the cost, since it varies with the exchange rate.

PASSPORT OFFICES

The best time to apply for a passport or to renew is in fall and winter. Before any trip, check your passport's expiration date and, if necessary, renew it as soon as possible.

➤ CANADIAN CITIZENS: **Passport Office** (tel. 819/994–3500 or 800/567–6868, www.dfait-maeci.gc.ca/passport).

➤ NEW ZEALAND CITIZENS: **New Zealand Passport Office** (tel. 04/494–0700, www.passports.govt.nz).

➤ U.K. CITIZENS: **London Passport Office** (tel. 0990/210–410) for fees and documentation requirements and to request an emergency passport.

➤ U.S. CITIZENS: **National Passport Information Center** (tel. 900/225–5674; calls are 35¢ per minute for automated service, $1.05 per minute for operator service).

Safety

Theft is the most likely problem you will encounter, and although crime rates are not high by world standards, you need to exercise caution. In major tourist areas such as Sydney's Bondi, the risk increases. When you park your vehicle, hide any valuables. Don't leave anything of value on the beach when you go for a swim. Under no conditions should you hitchhike.

Taxes

Everyone leaving Australia pays a departure tax (now known as a Passenger Movement Charge) of $27. This amount is prepaid with your airline ticket. Except for food, all goods and services incur a Goods and Services Tax (GST) of 10%.

Taxis

Taxis are a relatively economical way to cover short to medium distances in Sydney. A 3-km (2-mi) trip from Circular Quay to the eastern suburbs costs around $14. Drivers are entitled to charge more than the metered fare if the passenger's baggage exceeds 55 pounds, if the taxi has been booked by telephone, or if the passenger crosses Harbour Bridge, where a toll is levied. Fares are 10% higher between 10 pm and 5 am, when the numeral "2" will be displayed in the tariff indicator on the meter. At all other times, make sure the numeral "1" is displayed. Taxis are licensed to carry four passengers. Taxi stands can be found outside most bus and railway stations as well as outside the larger hotels. On the south side of the harbor, the most efficient telephone booking service is provided by Sydney Taxis. North of the bridge, try ABC Taxis.

➤ **Taxi Booking Services: Sydney Taxis** (tel. 13–1008). **ABC Taxis** (tel. 13–2522).

Telephones

Australia's telephone system is efficient and reliable. You can make long-distance and international calls from any phone in the country. Australian phone numbers have 8 digits.

Hotels impose surcharges that can double or even triple the cost of making calls from your room. Get around this by making calls from a public phone, or by charging to a local account (contact your local telephone service for details).

AREA & COUNTRY CODES

The country code for Australia is 61. From the U.S., dial 011, then 61, then the local area code. From the U.K., dial 00, then 61. When dialing an Australian number from abroad, drop the initial 0 from the local area code.

Area codes for the major cities are: Sydney and Canberra, 02; Melbourne and Hobart, 03; Brisbane and Cairns, 07; Adelaide, Darwin, and Perth, 08.

DIRECTORY & OPERATOR ASSISTANCE

For international directory assistance, call 1225. For information on international call costs, call 12552.

INTERNATIONAL CALLS

Calls from Australia to the United States, Canada, and the U.K. cost between 20¢ and $1 per minute (plus a 12¢ connection fee) in off-peak hours. These are weekdays 6 PM–9 AM, and all day on weekends. Operator-assisted calls can be made from any phone with IDD (International Direct Dialing) access. In Australia, a collect call is known as a "reverse-charge" call.

LOCAL CALLS

Australian numbers with a 13 prefix can be dialed country-wide for the cost of a local call, 40¢. Toll-free numbers in Australia have an 1800 prefix. Unless otherwise noted, toll-free numbers in this book are accessible only within Australia.

LONG-DISTANCE CALLS

Long-distance calls can be dialed directly using the city code or area code. A $3 service fee is charged for operator-connected calls when direct dialing is possible. Area codes are listed in the white pages of local telephone directories.

Since 1994, all telephone numbers in Australia have gradually been converted to eight-digit numbers. Exceptions are toll-free numbers and numbers with the prefix 13. When you're calling long-distance numbers within Australia, remember to include the area code, even when you are calling from a number with the same area code.

LONG-DISTANCE SERVICES

AT&T, MCI, and Sprint access codes make calling long distance relatively convenient, but you may find the local access number blocked in many hotel rooms. First ask the hotel operator to connect you. If the hotel operator balks, ask for an international operator, or dial the international operator yourself.

➤ **Access Codes: AT&T Direct** (tel. 800/435–0812). **MCI WorldPhone** (tel. 800/444–4141). **Sprint International Access** (tel. 800/877–4646).

PHONE CARDS

If you plan to make even a small number of phone calls, phone cards are a cost-efficient choice. Phone cards may be purchased from post offices or news agencies. They are available in units of $5, $10, $20, and $50. Most public phones will accept phone cards.

Time

Without daylight saving time, Sydney is 15 hours ahead of New York; 16 hours ahead of Chicago and Dallas; 18 hours ahead of Los Angeles; and 10 hours ahead of London.

Tipping

Hotels and restaurants do not add service charges, but it is a widely accepted practice to tip a waiter 10%–12% for good service, although many Australians consider it sufficient to leave only $3 or $4. It's not necessary to tip a hotel doorman for carrying suitcases into the lobby, but porters could be given $1 a bag. Room service and housemaids are not tipped except for special service. Taxi drivers do not expect a tip, but you may want to leave any small change. Guides, tour bus drivers, and chauffeurs don't expect tips either, though they are grateful if someone in the group takes up a collection for them. No tipping is necessary in beauty salons or for theater ushers.

Tours & Packages

Because everything is prearranged on a prepackaged tour or independent vacation, you'll spend less time planning—and often get it all at a good price.

Dozens of tour operators lead guided trips through Sydney and the surrounding areas. The Sydney Visitors Information Centre and other booking and information centers (☞ Visitor Information, *below*) can provide you with many more suggestions and recommendations.

BUYER BEWARE

Each year consumers are stranded or lose their money when tour operators go out of business. So **check out the operator.** Ask several travel agents about its reputation, and try to **book with a company that has a consumer-protection program.** In the United States, members of the National Tour Association and the United States Tour Operators Association are required to set aside funds to cover your payments and travel arrangements in the event that the company defaults. It's also a good idea to choose a company that participates in the American Society of Travel Agents' Tour Operator Program (TOP). ASTA will act as mediator in any disputes between you and your tour operator.

➤ **TOUR-OPERATOR RECOMMENDATIONS: American Society of Travel Agents** (☞ Travel Agencies, *below*). **National Tour Association (NTA)** (546 E. Main St., Lexington, KY 40508, tel. 606/226–4444 or 800/682–8886, www.ntaonline.com). **United States Tour Operators Association (USTOA)** (342 Madison Ave., Suite 1522, New York, NY 10173, tel. 212/599–6599 or 800/468–7862, fax 212/599–6744, www.ustoa.com).

Theme Trips

BOAT TOURS AND CRUISES

A replica of Captain Bligh's HMAV *Bounty* is alive and afloat on Sydney Harbour, and Bounty Cruises has various harbor excursions. Cruises depart from Campbell's Cove, in front of the Park Hyatt Sydney Hotel. The lunch cruise, which starts daily at

12:30, costs $55 ($80 weekend lunch), and the dinner cruise, daily at 7, will set you back $85.

The best introductory trip on Captain Cook Cruises (02/9206–1111) is the 2½-hour Coffee Cruise. The Sydney Harbour Explorer cruise allows you to disembark from the cruise boat, explore, and catch any following Captain Cook explorer cruise. Four Explorer cruises ($20) depart daily from Circular Quay at two-hour intervals, beginning at 9:30. Coffee cruises ($33) depart daily at 10 and 2:15. All cruises depart from Wharf 6, Circular Quay.

The State Transit Authority runs cruises aboard harbor ferries, at lower costs than those of privately operated cruises. All cruises depart from Wharf 4 at the Circular Quay terminal. The Morning Harbour Cruise is a one-hour cruise that takes in the major sights of the harbor to the east of the city. It costs $13 and departs daily at 10 and 11:15. The Afternoon Harbour Cruise ($19, departures at 1 on weekdays and 1:30 on weekends) is a leisurely 2½-hour tour that takes in the scenic eastern suburbs and affluent Middle Harbour. The 1½-hour Evening Harbour Lights Cruise takes you into Darling Harbour for a nighttime view of the city from the west, then passes the Garden Island naval base to view the Opera House and Kings Cross. The cruise departs Mon.–Sat. at 8 and costs $16.50.

➤ **BOAT TOUR OPERATORS: Bounty Cruises** (tel. 02/9247–1789); **Captain Cook Cruises** (tel. 02/9206–1111); **The State Transit Authority** (tel. 13–1500).

EXCURSIONS AND DAY TRIPS

Several coach companies run a variety of day trips in and around the Sydney region. There are city tours and excursions to such places as the Blue Mountains, the Hunter Valley wine region, Canberra, wildlife parks, and the 2000 Olympics site. The following operators have a 24-hour inquiry and reservation service.

➤ **DAY TOURS: AAT Kings** (tel. 02/9252–2788); **Australian Pacific Tours** (tel. 13–1304); **Murrays Australia** (tel. 02/9252–3590).

NATIONAL PARKS AND THE BUSH

Bush Limousine Tour Company specializes in small-group tours with an emphasis on quality. A choice of off-the-shelf or tailor-made tours is available to places such as the Blue Mountains, the Southern Highlands, the Hunter Valley, and the alpine region of southern New South Wales. Wild Escapes specializes in small-group ecotour and cultural excursions aboard four-wheel-drive vehicles, including trips to the Blue Mountains, the Hawkesbury River, the Hunter Valley, South Coast, and Olympic Park. Standard prices are about $190 for a full-day tour. Wildframe Eco Tours operates two one-day hiking-and-sightseeing trips to the Grand Canyon area. The price is $55, or $72 for a slightly less demanding walk.

➤ **CONTACT INFORMATION: Bush Limousine Tour Company** (tel. 02/9418–7826); **Wild Escapes** (tel. 02/9482–2881); **Wildframe Eco Tours** (tel. 02/9314–0658).

ORIENTATION TOURS

Tickets for either of the following State Transit Authority bus tours cost $28. They are valid for one day and can be purchased on board the buses or from the New South Wales Travel Centre.

The only guided bus tour of the inner city is the Sydney Explorer bus, which makes a 35-km (22-mi) circuit of all the major attractions in the city. The bright red buses follow one another every 20 minutes, and the service operates from 9 daily. The last bus to make the circuit departs Circular Quay at 5:25. The Bondi & Bay Explorer bus runs a guided bus tour of the eastern suburbs. The blue bus begins its 35-km (22-mi) journey at Circular Quay. Buses follow one another at 30-minute intervals beginning at 9. The last bus leaves at 4:20.

➤ **BUS TOUR INFORMATION: New South Wales Travel Centre.** (11–31 York St., tel. 13–2077).

WALKING TOURS

The Rocks Walking Tours offer introductions to the Rocks (the site of Sydney's original settlement by Europeans) with an emphasis on the buildings and personalities of the convict period. The tour, which lasts for 1½ hours and costs $11, travels at a gentle pace and involves little climbing. Weekday tours begin at 10:30, 12:30, and 2:30; weekend tours at 11:30 and 2.

Sydney Guided Tours with Maureen Fry are an excellent introduction to Sydney. Standard tours cost $17 and cover the colonial buildings along Macquarie Street, a ramble through the historic waterside suburbs of Glebe and Balmain or Circular Quay and the Rocks.

➤ **WALKING TOUR OPERATORS: The Rocks Walking Tours** (Kendall Lane, off Argyle St., the Rocks, tel. 02/9247–6678); **Sydney Guided Tours** (tel. 02/9660–7157, fax 02/9660–0805).

Train Travel

The monorail (tel. 02/9552–2288) is one of the fastest and most relaxing forms of public transport, but its use is limited to travel between the city center, Darling Harbour, and the Chinatown area. The flat-rate fare is $2.50, but $6 all-day passes are a better value if you intend to use the monorail to explore. The monorail operates every two–six minutes, generally from 7 AM to late evening, but times vary seasonally.

For journeys in excess of 7 km (4 mi), Sydney's trains are considerably faster than buses. However, the rail network has been designed primarily for rapid transit between outlying suburbs and the city. Apart from the City Circle line, which includes the Circular Quay and Town Hall stations and the spur line to Kings Cross and Bondi Junction, the system does not serve areas of particular interest to visitors. Travelers using trains should remember the following axioms: All trains pass through Central Station; Town Hall is the "shoppers" station;

the bus, ferry, and train systems converge at Circular Quay. Trains generally operate from 4:30 AM to midnight.

The Sydney Light Rail (tel. 02/9660–5288) is a limited system that provides a fast and efficient link between Central Station, Darling Harbour, and the Star City casino and entertainment complex. The modern, air-conditioned tram cars operate at 5- to 11-minute intervals, 24 hours per day. Round-trip tickets cost $3–$4.

Travel Agencies

A good travel agent puts your needs first. Look for an agency that has been in business at least five years, emphasizes customer service, and has someone on staff who specializes in your destination. In addition, **make sure the agency belongs to a professional trade organization.** The American Society of Travel Agents (ASTA), with 27,000 agents in some 170 countries, maintains a Web site that includes a directory of agents.

Scarcely a shopping plaza or main street in Sydney lacks a travel agency. Both American Express Travel Service and Thomas Cook are in the heart of the city, as well as in a number of suburbs.

➤ **LOCAL AGENT REFERRALS: American Express Travel Service** (92 Pitt St., tel. 02/9239–0666). **American Society of Travel Agents (ASTA)** (tel. 800/965–2782 24-hr hot line, fax 703/684–8319, www.astanet.com). **Association of British Travel Agents** (68–71 Newman St., London W1P 4AH, tel. 020/7637–2444, fax 020/7637–0713, www.abtanet.com). **Association of Canadian Travel Agents** (1729 Bank St., Suite 201, Ottawa, Ontario K1V 7Z5, tel. 613/521–0474, fax 613/521–0805). **Australian Federation of Travel Agents** (Level 3, 309 Pitt St., Sydney 2000, tel. 02/9264–3299, fax 02/9264–1085, www.afta.com.au). **Thomas Cook** (175 Pitt St., tel. 02/9231–2877). **Travel Agents' Association of New Zealand** (Box 1888, Wellington 10033, tel. 04/499–0104, fax 04/499–0827).

Visitor Information

For general information contact the national and regional tourism bureaus below. For a free information-packed booklet "Destination Australia," call tel. 800/333–0262. If you have specific questions about planning your trip, the Australian Tourism Commission runs the Aussie Help Line from 8 AM to 7 PM, Central Standard Time. Before you go, contact Friends Overseas—Australia to be put in touch with Australians who share your interests. Membership is $25.

There are also tourist information booths and more specialized tourist information centers throughout the city, including Circular Quay, Martin Place, Darling Harbour, and the Pitt Street Mall. The Backpacker's Travel Centre specializes in tours, accommodations, and information for the budget traveler. Countrylink, the state rail authority, is another source of Sydney and New South Wales travel information. The Sydney Information Line has useful recorded service and entertainment information.

➤ COUNTRYWIDE INFORMATION: **Aussie Help Line** (tel. 847/296–4900). **Australian Tourist Commission** US: (2049 Century Park E., Los Angeles, CA 90067, tel. 310/229–4870, fax 310/552–1215). U.K.: Gemini House, 10–18 Putney Hill, Putney, London SW15 6AA, tel. 0990/022–000 [information]; 0990/561–434 [brochure line], fax 020/8940–5221). New Zealand: (Level 13, 44–48 Emily Pl., Box 1666, Auckland 1, tel. 09/379–9594). **Backpacker's Travel Centre** (Shop 33, Imperial Arcade, off Pitt St. near Market St., tel. 02/9231–3699). **Countrylink** (11–31 York St., tel. 02/13–2077). **Friends Overseas—Australia** (68–01 Dartmouth St., Forest Hills, NY 11375, tel. 718/261–0534). **Sydney Information Line** (tel. 02/9265–9007). **Sydney Visitors Information Centre** (106 George St., the Rocks, tel. 02/9255–1788, fax 02/9241–5010). **Tourist Information Service** (tel. 02/9669–5111).

Web Sites

Do check out the World Wide Web when you're planning. You'll find everything from current weather forecasts to virtual tours of famous cities. Fodor's Web site, www.fodors.com, is a great place to start your online travels. For more specific information on Australia, visit Qantas (www.qantas.com.au) and Ansett (www.ansett.com/), the Web sites of Australia's two major airlines. Also try the New South Wales Government Web site (www.nsw.gov.au/).

When to Go

Australia is in the Southern Hemisphere, so **remember that the seasons are reversed.** It's winter Down Under during the American and European summer.

During school holidays, Australians take to the roads in droves; the busiest period is mid-December to the end of January, which is the equivalent of the U.S. and British summer break. The dates of other school vacations vary from state to state, but generally fall around Easter, mid-June to July, and late September to mid-October.

CLIMATE

Australia's climate is temperate in southern states, particularly in coastal areas. Remember that by comparison no parts of North America or Europe are anywhere near as close to the equator. From the end of October to December (the Australian spring), or from February through April (late summer–autumn), Sydney is generally sunny and warm, with only occasional rain. Some people would say that spring and fall are the best times to travel to Australia, unless you're dying to get away from a northern winter.

The following are average daily maximum and minimum temperatures for Sydney.

➤ **FORECASTS: Weather Channel Connection** (tel. 900/932–8437), 95¢ per minute from a Touch-Tone phone.

SYDNEY

Jan.	79F	26C	**May**	67F	19C	**Sept.**	67F	17C
	65	18		52	11		52	11
Feb.	79F	26C	**June**	61F	16C	**Oct.**	72F	22C
	65	18		49	9		56	13
Mar.	76F	24C	**July**	61F	16C	**Nov.**	74F	23C
	63	17		49	9		61	16
Apr.	72F	22C	**Aug.**	63F	17C	**Dec.**	77F	25C
	58	14		49	9		63	17

INDEX

A

Aboriginal art, 112
Admiralty House, 17
Air travel, 142–143
Airports and transfers, 143–144
AMP Tower, 58
Amusement parks, 55, 69, 72
ANA Hotel, 131–132
Andrew (Boy) Charlton Pool, 46
Anzac Memorial, 58–59
Aqua Luna, 88
Aquarium, 55–56
Argyle Cut, 25–26
Argyle Place, 26
Argyle Stairs, 25–26, 31
Argyle Stores, 26
Aria, 88–89
Army Museum, 67
Art galleries and museums, 28, 29, 37, 55
Art Gallery of New South Wales, 37
Arthur McElhone Reserve, 64
Arts, 123–129
ATMs, 156
Australian Museum, 58
Australian National Maritime Museum, 54
Australian Wildlife Park, 68
Australia's Wonderland, 68

B

Ballet, 123–124
Balmoral (beach), 77
Banc, 93
Bathers' Pavilion, 106
Bayswater Brasserie, 100
Beaches, 5, 76–77, 80–84
Beare Park, 64
Bel mondo, 88
Bennelong, 89
Bills, 95–96
Bistro Mars, 102–103
Bistro Moncur, 103
Boat and ferry travel, 144–145
Boat tours and cruises, 162–163
Boathouse on Blackwattle Bay, 106–107
Boating, 119
Bondi, 68–69
beach, 80–81
Bonne femme, 97–98
Bookshops, 112–113
Botany Bay, 81
Bridge Street, 40
Bronte (beach), 81

Brooklyn Bed and Breakfast, 141
Bungan (beach), 82
Buon Ricordo, 100
Bus travel, 145–146
Bush apparel and camping and outdoor gear, shopping for, 113
Business hours, 146

C

Cadman's Cottage, 27
Camp Cove (beach), 77, 80
Campbells Cove, 27
Car rentals, 146–147
Car travel, 147–148
Castlecrag, 15
Catalina Rose Bay, 103, 106
CDs and tapes, shopping for, 113
Centennial Park, 69
Chicane, 97
Chinese Garden, 54
Chinta Ria Temple of Love, 93–94
Chowder Bay, 16
Churches, 28, 41–42, 60
Circular Quay
dining, 87–89, 92
lodging, 131–133, 136–137
Circular Quay West, 30
City Center, 56–60
dining, 93–95
lodging, 137
Claude's, 102
Climate, 168–169
Clovelly (beach), 81
Coast, 94–95
Collaroy-Narrabeen (beach), 82–83
Colonial Secretary's Office, 40
Comedy clubs, 126
Consulates, 152–153
Coogee (beach), 81
Craft shops, 113–114
Credit cards, 156
Cricket, 117
Cronulla (beach), 82
Currency exchange, 156–157
Customs, 148–151
Customs House, 38

D

Dance, 124
Darling Harbour, 50–51, 54–56
Darlinghurst, 61–67
dining, 95–100
Dawes Point Park, 27
Dee Why-Long Reef, 83
Department stores, 109
Dining, 5–6, 151–152
City Center, 93–95
East Sydney and Darlinghurst, 95–100
Kings Cross, 100
Paddington, 100–101
Potts Point, 101
price categories, 87
the Rocks and Circular Quay, 87–89, 92
Sydney area, 102–103, 106–107

Discounts and deals, 152
Domain North, 44–50
Domain South, 32–44
Double Bay Bed and Breakfast, 139–140
Doyle's on the Beach, 107
Dragonfly, 98
Duties, 148–151
Duty-free shops, 109–110

E

East Sydney
dining, 95–100
lodging, 138–140
Electricity, 152
Elizabeth Bay, 61–67
Elizabeth Bay House, 64
Embassies and consulates, 152–153
Emergencies, 153–154
Exploring
City Center, 56–60
Darling Harbour, 50–51, 54–56
Elizabeth Bay and Kings Cross, Darlinghurst, and Paddington, 61–67
Macquarie Street and the Domain South, 32–44
Opera House, the RBG, and the Domain North, 44–50
the Rocks and Sydney Harbour Bridge, 20–32
Sydney area, 67–69, 72–76
Sydney Harbour, 11–20

F

Farm Cove, 16
Featherdale Wildlife Park, 69
Ferry travel, 144–145
Fishface, 99
Flea markets, 110–111
Football, 118
Fort Denison, 16
Forty One, 94
Fox Studios, 69, 72
Freshwater (beach), 83
Fuel, 98
Fu-Manchu, 96

G

Gambling, 126
Garden Island, 16–17
Garden Palace Gates, 38
Gardens, 16, 44–50, 54
Gay bars and clubs, 127
Golden Century, 93
Golf, 118
Government House, 47–48
Grace Hotel, 137
Gumnut Café, 29–30

H

Harbour Rocks Hotel, 136
Harbourkitchen & bar, 89, 92
Harrington Street, 28
Harry's Café de Wheels, 65
Hero of Waterloo, 28–29
History House, 38
Holy Trinity Church, 28
Hotel Inter-Continental Sydney, 132
Hughenden, 138
Hugo's, 107

Hyde Park, 58–59
Hyde Park Barracks, 39
Hyde Park Barracks Café, 39

I

IMAX Theatre, 54–55

J

Jazz clubs, 127–128
Jersey Cow, 101
Juniper Hall, 65

K

Kings Cross, 61–67
dining, 100
Kirribilli, 17
Knitwear shops, 114
Koala Park Sanctuary, 72
Ku-ring-gai Chase National Park, 72–73

L

La Mensa, 100–101
Lady Jane (beach), 80
Lands Department, 39
Language, 154
Library, 42
Lodging, 154–155
City Center, 137
east of the city, 138–140
in Paddington and Woollahra, 138
price categories, 131
the Rocks and Circular Quay, 131–133, 136–137
Sydney area, 140–141
Longrain, 99
Lord Nelson (pub), 26
Lower Fort Street, 28

M

Macquarie Place, 39–40
Macquarie Street, 32–44
Mail and shipping, 155
Manly, 73–74
beach, 83
Marble Bar, 59
Maroubra (beach), 82
Marque, 96
Martin Place, 59
MCA Café, 92
Medical plans, 154
Medusa, 139
MG Garage Restaurant, 97
Middle Harbour, 17
Middle Head, 17
Money matters, 155–157
Mrs. Macquarie's Chair, 46
Mrs. Macquarie's Point, 46–47
Museum of Contemporary Art, 29
Museum of Sydney, 40
Museums. ☞ Art galleries and museums
Australian history, 38
banking, 32
in City Center, 58
in Darling Harbour, 54, 55
in Elizabeth Bay and Kings Cross, Darlinghurst, and Paddington, 66, 67
Jewish culture, 66

in Macquarie Street and the Domain South area, 38, 40
maritime history, 54
military, 67
natural history, 58
in the Rocks area, 32
science, 55
Sydney history, 40
Music, 43, 123–124, 127–129

N

National parks, 6, 72–73, 74–75, 164
Newport (beach), 83
Nielsen Park (beach), 80
Nightclubs, 128–129
Nightlife and the arts, 123–129
Nurses Walk, 28, 29

O

Observatory, 31
Observatory Hill, 30
Observatory Hotel, 132–133
Olympic Games site, 75–76
Opal shops, 114
Opera, 123–124
Opera House, 44–50
Orientation tours, 164
Outback Woolshed, 68
Outdoor activities, 7, 117–120
Overseas Passenger Terminal, 30

P

Packing, 157
Paddington, 61–67
dining, 100–101
lodging, 138
Palm Beach, 83–84
Panasonic IMAX Theatre, 54–55
Paramount, 101
Park Hyatt Sydney, 133
Parks
City Center, 58–59
Elizabeth Bay and Kings Cross, Darlinghurst, and Paddington, 64
Macquarie Street and the Domain South area, 38
national parks, 6, 72–73, 74–75, 164
the Rocks, 27
Sydney area, 69, 72–73, 74–76
Passports, 157–158
Pier, 107
Point Piper, 17
Potts Point, 101
Powerhouse Museum, 55
Prasit's Northside on Crown, 99–100
Price categories
for dining, 87
for lodging, 131
Prime, 95
Pubs, 129
Pyrmont Bridge, 55

Q

Quarantine Station, 18
Quay, 87–88
Queen Victoria Building, 59–60
Quick tours, 7–9

R

Ravesi's on Bondi Beach, 140
Regent of Sydney, 133, 136

Ritz-Carlton, Sydney, 136
Rockpool, 89
the Rocks, 20–32
dining, 87–89, 92
lodging, 131–133, 136–137
Rocks Police Station, 29
Rose Bay, 18
Royal Australasian College of Physicians, 40
Royal Botanic Gardens (RBG), 16, 44–50
Royal National Park, 74–75
Running, 118–119
Russell, 137

S

S. H. Ervin Gallery, 28
Safety, 158
Sailing, 119
Sailor's Thai, 92
St. Andrew's Cathedral, 60
St. James Church, 41
St. Mary's Cathedral, 41–42
Salt, 97
Scuba diving, 119, 153
Sean's Panorama, 102
Sebel of Sydney, 138–139
Sega World, 55
Shadforth Street, 66
Shelly (beach), 84
Shimbashi Soba, 103
Shopping, 7, 109–115
Simpsons of Potts Point, 139
South East Pylon, 31
Sports, 7, 117–120
Stafford Apartments Sydney, 136–137
State Library of New South Wales, 42
State Parliament House, 43
Suez Canal, 28, 30
Sullivans Hotel, 138
Summit, 94
Surfing, 119–120
Sydney Aquarium, 55–56
Sydney area, 67–69, 72–76
dining, 102–103, 106–107
lodging, 140–141
Sydney Conservatorium of Music, 43
Sydney Cove, 18
Sydney Harbour, 11–20
Sydney Harbour Bridge, 30–31
Sydney Hospital, 43–44
Sydney Jewish Museum, 66
Sydney Mint, 44
Sydney Observatory, 31
Sydney Olympic Park, 75–76
Sydney Opera House, 44–50
Sydney Town Hall, 60
Sydney Visitors Information Centre, 31–32

T

Tamarama (beach), 82
Taronga Zoo, 18–19
Taxes, 158–159
Taxis, 159
Telephones, 159–161

Tennis, 120
Tetsuya's, 106
Theater, 124–125
Theme trips, 162–165
Time, 161
Timing the visit, 9, 168–169
Tipping, 161
Tours and packages, 161–162
Train travel, 165–166
Travel agencies, 166
Traveler's checks, 157
Treasury Building, 40
Trickett's, 140–141
T-shirts and beachwear, shopping for, 115

U

Upper George Street, 32

V

Vaucluse, 19
Victoria Barracks, 66–67
Victoria Court Sydney, 140
Visas, 157–158
Visitor information, 31–32, 167

W

Walking tours, 165
Warriewood (beach), 84
Watsons Bay, 19–20
Web sites, 168
Westpac Banking Museum, 32
When to go, 9, 168–169
Wildlife preserves, 6, 68, 69, 72
William Bligh statue, 26
Windsurfing, 120
Wockpool, 95
Woollahra, 138

Z

Zoo, 18–19

FODOR'S POCKET SYDNEY

EDITORS: Amy Karafin, Jennifer L. Kasoff, Holly S. Smith

EDITORIAL CONTRIBUTORS: Michael Gebicki, Terry Durack

EDITORIAL PRODUCTION: Kristin Milavec

MAPS: David Lindroth, *cartographer*; Bob Blake and Rebecca Baer, *map editors*

DESIGN: Fabrizio La Rocca, *creative director*; Tigist Getachew, *art director*

PRODUCTION/MANUFACTURING: Robert B. Shields/Yexenia Markland

COVER PHOTOGRAPH: Roger Garwood & Trish Ainslie/Corbis

COPYRIGHT

ISBN 0-679-00686-9

ISSN 1523-9446

IMPORTANT TIP

Although all prices, opening times, and other details in this book are based on information supplied to us at press time, changes occur all the time in the travel world, and Fodor's cannot accept responsibility for facts that become outdated or for inadvertent errors or omissions. So **always confirm information when it matters,** especially if you're making a detour to visit a specific place.

SPECIAL SALES

Fodor's Travel Publications are available at special discounts for bulk purchases for sales promotions or premiums. Special editions, including personalized covers, excerpts of existing guides, and corporate imprints, can be created in large quantities for special needs. For more information, contact your local bookseller or write to Special Markets, Fodor's Travel Publications, 280 Park Avenue, New York, NY 10017. Inquiries from Canada should be directed to your local Canadian bookseller or sent to Random House of Canada, Ltd., Marketing Department, 2775 Matheson Boulevard East, Mississauga, Ontario L4W 4P7. Inquiries from the United Kingdom should be sent to Fodor's Travel Publications, 20 Vauxhall Bridge Road, London SW1V 2SA, England.

PRINTED IN THE UNITED STATES OF AMERICA

10 9 8 7 6 5 4 3 2 1